CHILDREN of
DISOBEDIENCE

CHILDREN of DISOBEDIENCE

*The Love Story of Martin Luther
and Katharina von Bora*

A Novel by
ASTA SCHEIB

Translated by David Ward

A Crossroad Book
The Crossroad Publishing Company
New York

First Published in the U.S.A. in 2000 by
The Crossroad Publishing Company
370 Lexington Avenue, New York, N.Y. 10017

Original Edition 1985 Kinder des Ungehorsams by Asta Scheib
Published by Nymphenburger Verlagshandlung, Munich

Printed in the United States of America

Library of Congress Cataloging-in-Publication Data
Scheib, Asta.
[Kinder des Ungehorsams.   English]
Children of disobedience : the love story of Martin Luther
and Katharina von Bora / by Asta Scheib :
translated by David Ward
p.   cm.
ISBN 0-8245-1695-8
1. Luther, Martin, 1483-1546—Fiction.   2. Luther, Katharina
von Bora, 1499-1552—Fiction.   I. Ward, David.
II. Title.
PT2638.E336K5613   2000
833'.914—DC21   97-33475
                                                                      CIP

1   2   3   4   5   6   7   8   9   10   04   03   02   01   00

CHILDREN of
DISOBEDIENCE

1

———

"*Katharina, I'm afraid.*"

"So am I, Ave."

The cell is unusually dark. This Easter night, the night between the fourth and the fifth of April in the year 1523, this night sends only a little light through the small, four-paned cell window. It's cold. Too cold for this time of year. Is that the punishment? Katharina feels the shivering about to come over her again. "There will be weeping and gnashing of teeth." Just don't lose your head now. Not tonight.

"I'm cold," whispers Ave.

Katharina rolls noiselessly out of bed. She has learned to do this. Without making a sound she slips in next to Ave, who holds open the covers like the door of a bedchamber. The door of a hiding place. Tenderly they wrap their arms around each other. As they have on so many other nights. But on this night they are wearing veil, habit, and belt. Ready to flee.

Ave squeezes Katharina's hand tightly. "Do you think the Devil will come to take us?"

Katharina replies fiercely, "If we stay here, the Devil will take us for sure."

The two girls lie still again, listening. Since four o'clock in the morning they have been awake, like every morning, when from the ridge turret the bell calls everyone to Angelus Domini. Most of them still drugged with sleep, they whoosh from the darkness of the dormitory through the cloister passageway to the house of God. The Psalms, invoked day after day, slip from their lips by themselves: "I walk before the Lord in the land of the living."

The other nuns are already sitting in the choir. In the candlelit dusk of the church, they seem to bob up and down like black-headed pigeons. Like the quiet rushing of waters come the waves: "God, attend to my aid, Lord, hasten to help me."

That has been the start of Katharina's day. For nearly twenty years. Until this night.

"Help me, Lord!" Once again the burning fear comes over her. In just a little while, when the signal is given, she and Ave and the others will run away from this cloister. The plan, arranged down to the smallest detail, now strikes Katharina as insane. Kidnapping nuns or abetting their flight is punishable by death. What if Leonhard Koppe loses his courage? He is a city councillor and tax receiver in Torgau. A treasury official of the Saxon elector's who helps women of holy orders escape from their cloisters. Will he keep his word?

"Katharina, do you hear it?"

Ave has sat up in bed. Now Katharina, too, is listening intently. An owl is screeching in the nearby woods. That's them. Koppe, his nephew Leonhard, and Wolf Dommitzsch, also a councillor in Torgau.

"Hurry!" Katharina takes Ave's hand.

The two of them steal out of the cell. There come Veronika and Else from the next cell. Across the way, Magdalene and Laneta have already reached the door that opens onto the garden. If the dormitory weren't in the back of the cloister, if there weren't a door leading from the dormitory into the cloister garden, if the cloister garden didn't border on the cloister woodlands, if, if, if . . .

All nine of them are in the garden now. Ave Grosse is already over among the trees. In their loose white habits they all hurry and stumble across the few yards separating them from the little woods. Thank God! Evidently no one has seen them. No one speaks as they trudge on, as fast as they can manage, through the dense forest. It is dark. They could use a torch. But that would be madness. Katharina pulls Ave along behind her. She picks her way through the dense undergrowth.

Now they have reached the pond. The surface of the water glistens silver-gray through the trees. Keep going. They won't be safe until they are inside Koppe's covered wagon. At any second their disappearance could be discovered in the cloister. The bell could sound, calling out Thalheim the gatekeeper.

Everyone would wake up. The people in the brewing house, in the baking house, in the slaughterhouse. The ones in the smithy and those in the mill. The provost in the provostry with the bailiff and the scribe. The two fathers confessor—they would all search the little woods first.

Faster, still faster. Through the trees Katharina sees the little house of the woodcutter-stoker. That man, whose sooty hands make the cloister ovens glow and roar, he would put the others off the track . . . His house stands quiet and dark. Abreast of this section of the woods lies the cloister estate, with its outlying properties and the six small farms that belong to them. Here is where the field laborers live, the cow- and swineherds, the dairywomen and maids who serve the cloister. A great flock of sheep belongs to the cloister and at least sixty head of cattle. Thirty horses and a hundred pigs. Only forty pigs just now, because of a recent outbreak of swine plague. Everything that can be seen from the central buildings belongs to the cloistered virgins. The wreath of hamlets, estates, and outlying farms on all sides of the cloister is its life-giving frame. "Give the emperor what belongs to him and give God what belongs to God." Katharina knows that along with the wheat and rye, the peas and turnips, along with hemp, flax, and hops, a large and growing portion of bitterness and hostility is being delivered to the cloister. The peasants, whose feudal obligations require these payments, no longer hand over the butter, the eggs, the chickens and capons willingly. There are more and more signs of unrest and hatred toward the nuns and the clergy.

✦　✦　✦

Now, as Katharina rushes breathlessly through the woods, as she sees the peasants' houses silent and unprotected in the darkness, she is reminded of that Saturday in February.

The sisters are sitting in the refectory. The Reverend Mother is serving the soup. Everyone spoons her soup in silence. There, coming from the provostry, first a murmur and a thump, then loud, rough voices, coarse shouting. Above it all the voice of Gatekeeper Thalheim: "Out, you dogs, get out of here!"

Katharina sees the Domina's face freeze for a moment. Then the Reverend Mother gets to her feet. "Stay calm, children. I'll be right back."

But already they've begun rushing in, at their head Ulrich Schmid and Hans Galster along with hunchbacked Jobst Weissbrod and Lazarus Ebner. Katharina sees that they are wearing their best clothes. And now Katharina Ebnerin and Klara, Galster's wife, crowd in among the three men who stand before the Reverend Mother. The women's voices tremble both with long pent-up anger and with fear: "Release us from the feudal rent, Reverend Mother!"

It almost seems that Ebnerin is startled at her own courage. But Galsterin quickly adds: "We're not giving you any more chickens and hens and eggs."

Ebnerin: "And our men shouldn't have to serve you any more. You've worked us to the bone and then some."

Now the men push ahead of the women. But before they can say anything, the Domina has regained her composure: "I do not have the authority to diminish that which is the cloister's. It disturbs me that you assume I would. Nevertheless—let me see how the other cloisters are dealing with their subordinates. And, incidentally, I do not have the feeling that I am burdening you so unbearably that you need to make such a commotion and stir up the others against us. I ask you to stop it, so that the cloister, and all of us with it, may not fall into misfortune."

At first, the others are still. But then they all begin to talk at once. Men and women: they speak of Adam and Moses. About how everyone who has an easy life in the cloister should work, too, not just peasants. And that they're not going to spread the manure, mow, or cut anymore. They aren't going to bring in the grain and thresh it anymore. They won't pick hops for the cloister's beer anymore. They won't pluck or ret the flax and hemp anymore. They won't dig up weeds anymore. They won't chop firewood for the nuns anymore. Nor clear mud and ice from the mill-race anymore. Nor shear the hundreds of sheep anymore.

The people talk themselves more and more into a rage.

Even before the Domina can give a response, Thalheim plants himself between the Reverend Mother and the peasants: "I am a simple man and I can't write one letter. Same as all of you. I can't tell you much about the Bible, either. But I will tell you one thing. You are wrong! It is written: Give to Caesar what belongs to Caesar and to God what belongs to God."

And with the help of the provost and the scribes, who have arrived in the meanwhile, he is able to send the peasants back home.

This time they go away with only angry words. But on the second Sunday of Lent, March 19, they are back again. And on the Monday after Mid-Lent Sunday, March 27, they return with a horse and wagon. They take the grain, the cider, the beer, and a lot of dried meat. The steward trembles with rage as he reports this to the Domina. The Reverend Mother leaves the cloister proper, motioning the prioress and the subprioress to accompany her into the courtyard. Katharina, Laneta, Ave, and Else run after the sisters. (In the excitement nobody stops them.) In the courtyard, a number of peasants with their wives are busy carrying off sacks, bottles, and bowls. Thalheim bellows, "You'll all wind up on the gallows, you filthy rabble. Just wait until the bishop hears about this, and the elector! You'll all hang!"

The Galsterin woman walks right up to the Domina. Her gaunt face is bright red. She screams, "We won't go on eating cabbage every day! We want to eat our fish, our chickens, and our butter ourselves! And instead of water on Sundays, we want to drink the cider that we pressed. It all belongs to us! And the Devil will come and take you, not us. Luther said so."

Ebnerin screams even louder: "We want to be ladies just like you! And if you have our men killed, we will strangle you. *You* go out into the fields and into the stalls, go ahead! Put on our scratchy jerkins and milk the cows. And we'll sit in the cloister and pray and wear warm furs. We're going to take you to the whores and we're going to tie your white robes over your heads! And then let the men have at you! You'll have babies and labor pains just like we do!"

How white the Reverend Mother's face is. She says not one word. Turns around and walks away. Everyone stands gaping after her. The peasants and their wives leave the cloister courtyard as well.

The subprioress has red splotches on her throat. She fumes, "There you have it, children, that's the fruit of the new gospel. Obey no one, rise up and rebel everywhere, gather together in mobs, plunder and murder both religious and worldly authority."

"Please be quiet," says the Mother Abbess.

Katharina will never forget the white face of the Reverend Mother.

Why was there no anger in her eyes? Why didn't she have the peasants punished? Why didn't she even inform Abbot Peter? Again the thought occurs to Katharina that the Domina . . .

✦　✦　✦

No, the idea is absurd. It's Katharina's own fear, her constant self-doubts, that have prompted such thoughts. When the Reverend Mother discovers her nuns' flight, when she realizes that nine of her children are breaking their vows . . . "Sweet Mother of God, help!"

Finally the girls tumble out of the sheltering forest. Before them lies the road to Grimma. This is where Leonhard Koppe is supposed to be waiting with the wagon. But where is he? They all crowd around Katharina, out of breath from rushing through the forest, shaking with fright. What if Koppe doesn't come? What if at the last minute he doesn't comply with Luther's request? Laneta von Gohlis begins sobbing aloud. "Quiet. I hear footsteps." In the night's indistinct light they make out the figure of a man who until now has been hidden in the bushes.

"I am Koppe. In the name of Luther. Come quickly."

Two men, the younger Koppe and Wolfgang Dommitzsch, cautiously steer a covered wagon out from the shadows at the edge of the woods. They help the girls up.

Terrified and exhausted, the girls huddle together on a thick layer of straw covered with sacks. The three men climb into the driving box. They draw the canvas tight in front as well.

"Holy Mother Mary, thank you."

They sob, cry, and pray all at once. Then they are still. There is only the creaking and jogging of the wagon, the clip-clop of the horses' hooves. Else von Canitz vomits.

"She's spewing the Devil out of her," says Ave.

"No fighting now," pleads Veronika von Zeschau. They are all tired, and all they really want is to sleep. But the bumping and jostling are too great. And so is the fear.

✦ ✦ ✦

Easter Monday in Torgau

Out in the world, will I become a different person? Katharina doesn't know whether she dreamed this sentence or not. At the border between sleep and waking, where joy—but fear and grief as well—can stir the soul so forcefully that one is unable to distinguish between what is dreamed and what is real, there she saw the fires of Purgatory. Or what else was it?

Katharina cannot wake up from her dream. Although she wants to, it holds her in its grip. She has dreamed of Martin Luther. From the narratives of Margarete and Veronika, whose uncle has seen him often, an image of the famous reformer has taken shape in Katharina's head. She has heard that he has fiery eyes, a gaunt body exhausted by worries and studies. That he refutes his enemies with a sharp, deliberate voice. They say he does it more casually and cuttingly than befits a theologian.

In her dream she sees Martin Luther riding on horse-back across the cloister cemetery. His horse is pale in the moonlight, but it does have an ornate bridle. Luther is hurdling the gravestones. His sword is drawn. Behind him comes an army of the dead, dressed in their shrouds. Katharina sees Ave, Veronika, Margarete, Else, and the others among the dead. They are armed with axes, scythes, and clubs. Their skulls are laughing. She herself, Katharina, carries a lance. Soldiers and peasants are in the way; they beg for mercy. Katharina feels fear even after she awakes. Does the dream mean that they are all going to die with Luther?

Restlessly Katharina tosses and turns on her straw mattress. The others should wake up now, too. She doesn't want to think about it anymore. If only she and Ave had run off by themselves. Now she is stuck with these others, too. Katharina forgets for a moment that without Veronika and Margarete von Zeschau things would probably have remained just as they were. Hadn't their uncle, the noble-man Wolfgang von Zeschau, smuggled Luther's writings into the cloister again and again? Where else would they have discovered the truth? Only last year he, the prior of the Augustinian monastery in Grimma, left the order along with several of the brothers. Now he is master of the Holy Cross *Spital* in Grimma, run by the Order of St. John of Jerusalem. He used to visit his nieces regularly, and he never came empty-handed.

What a day, when he brought the first pamphlet!

Margarete carries four texts out of the visiting room.

She has concealed the rolls easily in the loose sleeves of her robe. Oh, they are good at hiding things. And at finding hiding places, where with burning cheeks and ears they read *The Sermon on Good Works*, *Address to the Christian Nobility*, *On the Babylonian Captivity of the Church*, *On the Freedom of a Christian* . . .

By this time, Luther is familiar to all of them. He sits with them in the choir at the Angelus, he does the reading at table, he praises God at the None. Everyone knows that the papal ban hangs menacingly over Luther's head. Officially, his name may not be mentioned in the cloister. But Katharina knows that the Domina studies his writings behind locked doors. And she also knows where these writings are kept. Every time the Reverend Mother goes to Torgau with the prioress and the subprioress to settle accounts with the city councillors and to buy supplies for the cloister, Katharina sits with pounding heart and hammering temples, reading about the great struggle that a monk began and that now is progressing with tremendous force. The upper classes and the common people have both risen up to quarrel with this monk.

Martin Luther. Katharina has many pictures of him in her head. They keep changing. From Luther's writings she knows the little Martin sitting in his parents' home and struggling with a Latin primer. He knows he's in for a sound beating if he can't do the conjugations. Martin is afraid of school. Often, he can't keep his thoughts together. Declension, syntax, meter, blows, fear, misery.

Father, I love you. The beatings hurt, Father. I'll learn my lesson better tomorrow, Father. Mother, is mean old Alp going to come after me, is he going to squash my heart? Tell me the story of the good elves, Mother, can I have one of those caps, too—the kind that make you invisible? Then the wicked witches won't be able to find me and put a spell on me, right, Mother? Then they won't be able to do anything to me. Mother, is it true that Klara Nutzlin put a curse on our sister? Is that why she screamed herself to death? Did she send the hail, and suck out all the cows' milk? Mother, can she ride through the air at night? Can she choke me until I don't get any air, *Mother*?

Katharina knows what frightened the young Luther in the night, and on dark days. She, too, has sat with heart pounding as she listened to Sister Angela describe the haunted forest in all its details: there they squatted on the ground, witches young and old, with breasts full or sagging. They were pounding poisonous herbs with mortar and pestle, preparing magic potions they would use to despoil man and beast. With terrifying songs and shrill laughter they rode naked through the air. They took away little girls in order to make them into witches and consecrate them forever to Hell.

Fear, blind obedience, punishment. That is the world of Katharina's childhood as well. She is five years old and she stares at the wooden door, the bolt of which is just being slid shut. She is not allowed to go out. She doesn't want to, either. Out there, fear lurks in every nook and cranny. It's dark and cold out there. Mother isn't here anymore. The many folds of her skirt no longer rustle through the house. Her footstep no longer resounds on the plank floors. Her soft arms no longer enfold Katharina. Mother is lying in the front room. They haven't let Katharina go to her there. For two days now. As usual, Katharina gets to stay with the chickens in the yard. But she hears none of their noise. The sun traces shadows on the sandy earth, but inside Katharina is not warmed. Mother. There is such a silence in the house. Then whispering, again, that quickly falls silent when Katharina enters the room.

Outside now, the cart is clattering and bouncing away. Katharina could climb up onto the wooden sill, squeeze way into the deep window well. She could look out. Katharina wants to and she doesn't want to. She feels like crying. But there is a stone inside her. It is lodged at the top of her throat and won't let the tears out.

The other woman with the other skirts sleeps with Father now. She doesn't have soft arms. Just hard hands. She gets Katharina dressed for the journey.

"You will go to the convent," says her father. "That's a big house with lots of women and girls. And God lives there."

Katharina knows God. Sometimes he walks around in Heaven with his big boots, and then there's thunder and lightning. Katharina didn't used to be afraid of that. Mother's warm, soft back was the answer to all questions, protection from all fear.

Katharina's new dress scratches against her skin, the belt is tight. She feels only this discomfort as they lift her onto the wagon. Father sits in silence. So does the woman. Katharina really needs to go to the bathroom. The woman reminded her to go before they left. Now the water is straining Katharina's bladder, but she won't say anything.

She is dizzy from the jostling of the wagon, from itching, from the pressure in her bladder. Katharina presses her lips together tight. Furtively she wedges one foot between her thighs. No one can see it beneath her long skirt.

The coach bumps and jostles Katharina into a near sleep, from which she suddenly wakes when something hot runs down her legs. Her heart pounds, her head seems to be bursting. She looks at Father, but he has nodded off, his head bobs back and forth. But the woman. She has seen it. She looks at Katharina with the look she always has when Father isn't there. The woman looks and doesn't speak and her mouth is narrow. Katharina adjusts her things amid the unpleasant wetness. From now on, she will not pray for the woman. Never again.

✦ ✦ ✦

In the midst of all these memories, Katharina has fallen asleep again. She has dreamt of her mother, as happens frequently. Every time, Katharina awakes with a strong, painfully sweet feeling of love. Then she is in a soft, tender mood . . . In the sleeping room, meanwhile, daylight is pouring in. The maid has just come in to clean out the stove and light it anew. The young girl is wearing a bright apron over a coarse brown shift. A red scarf is tied around her head. Now she plants her fists on her hips. "So, did you sleep this late in the convent, too?"

Grumbling under her breath, she gets to work at the stove, sweeps out the soot, making lots of clatter and dust.

Now they are all awake. "Oh, God, what will the day bring us?" Else von Canitz worries aloud. Katharina's soft mood is gone instantly. Let the Devil take them all! Except Ave, of course.

The others annoy her with their constant bawling, blubbering, and bickering. Else especially. False as the serpent in Eden. Constantly having fits of hysteria. She stuffs huge quantities of food into herself. Then she throws it all back up. Over and over again. No one wants to share a room with her. Else wasn't supposed to come with them. But she overheard everything. Katharina looks at Else. The restless eyes of the nineteen-year-old are reddened now. So is her nose. Clearly, she has caught cold. Katharina feels feverish, too. Running through the woods yesterday, then lying drenched with sweat in the wagon. The cold air. Katharina's head feels heavy, dull. That's all she needs, to get sick now! Laneta beside her coughs, and Margarete complains of a sore throat. Councillor Koppe will be grateful. Nine runaway nuns in his house, and all of them sick.

"A fine bunch of Easter lambs you are." The maid says this as she leaves. She holds the door open for Walpurga, Leonhard Koppe's wife. Walpurga asks how the young ladies have slept. And now, she says, they should come into the main room for the morning meal. Over a white chemise, Walpurga Koppe wears a dress of the finest blue fabric. With it, a white bonnet with a ribbon on each side, pulled rather far down over her forehead. She sits at the lower end of the oaken dining table. To the left, a dark green tiled stove spreads cozy warmth. It is hexagonal and has splendidly decorated relief tiles. Katharina praises its beauty, and Walpurga says with pride that a famous stove fitter from Italy came and built it just a year ago.

Councillor Koppe summons everyone to table. This is actually the first time the girls have seen him by daylight. Koppe is a stocky man in his fifties. His clean-shaven face is fleshy, his mouth energetic. The children and the servants hang on his every gesture.

Now the children file silently onto the benches at table. It's a rather cheerful silence, though: Katharina sees furtive glances, repressed laughter. Koppe gives the signal for the blessing, which the youngest son rattles off, his eyes intently lowered. Suddenly, Katharina is feeling very hungry. The spiced bread is good. There are even white breakfast rolls. And with them almond-flavored milk and fresh cream. Also a porridge of crushed oats and whole-grain cereal. One of the children gives a yelp. He has broken a tooth. There was a piece of rock in the bread. Walpurga turns to the maid, who is serving, and asks sternly, "Did you forget to sift the flour again? I've told you a thousand times, you have to sift it three times to remove the bits of millstone. You useless creature! Do you want all our teeth to fall out?"

"One more time, and you can pack your things." With this threat, the councillor brings his wife's burst of anger to a close.

Katharina is not sorry to see the sharp-tongued maid get her due. Especially since she has bitten into a large, black stone herself. Not too firmly, though. Ave Grosse, also, chews cautiously on her mouthful and then wordlessly lays a little stone beside her plate.

After the morning meal, they will be on their way to Wittenberg. But what are the girls to put on? As runaways, they certainly can't go on wearing the attire of their order. The councillor's wife regrets that she has not been able to come up with clothing for the girls. No one wants to give anything. She herself might have something for one of the girls to wear, but that's all. So they are left with the white habits. The belts and veils they all take off. They look comical enough as it is, with their short, stubbly, matted hair. Gently, Walpurga says, "Wouldn't you rather keep the veil on for now?"

The girls look to Katharina. She crumples up her veil and hurls it to the floor. She is almost shouting: "The special sanctity of this veil is no longer ours to wear. Luther has torn it from our heads."

Everyone is silent. The maid brings warm shawls and blankets. With these they cover up as best they can, as they climb back into the covered wagon for the wintry journey to Wittenberg.

Near the Koppe house stands Torgau's church. Katharina would have liked to go inside, to thank God for their successful escape. But it is still too dangerous. The church stands under the patronage of the Marienthron cloister, and no one knows yet whether the Mother Abbess will have her escaped nuns pursued. So Katharina sends wordless thanks to the house of God. She cannot know that it is here, where her actual life is beginning, that she will be buried thirty years hence.

✦　✦　✦

When the covered wagon arrives in Wittenberg, it attracts much attention. Thank Heaven Torgau is not as far as from

Wittenberg as the Marienthron cloister is from Torgau. Still, the girls are utterly exhausted. They feel dirty. Laneta's and Else's faces are bright red from fighting. The two have really gone after each other again. But now they are all still, looking anxiously out at the staring crowd that surrounds the wagon. More and more people arrive. Students in uniform, daggers in their belts. There are boys no more than twelve years old, and men around forty. Three *Doctores* wearing red birettas oversee the students. Market women leave their vegetables and chickens and come running. The students avail themselves of the opportunity to steal. Journeyman craftsmen come and stand gaping.

Mortified with embarrassment, the girls brush the straw from their clothing.

"Hey you, is it liberties you've come for—or lover boys?" One of the students shouted this, and they all laugh.

"Luther says the holy virgins are really Satan's virgins."

Leonhard Koppe, who is shepherding the girls toward the home of Lucas Cranach as quickly as possible, is angry. He takes a few steps toward the shouter. "You are so stupid and such a hypocrite, they ought to stick you on the spit at some convent and roast your ass."

✦   ✦   ✦

The girls are sitting in the ornately crafted, paneled living room of Lucas Cranach, feeling utterly lost. Cranach's wife, Barbara, hurries in with a maid. She serves her new guests water, wine, and bread.

Cranach is a tall, fine-featured man in his fifties. He has bright green eyes with a lively sparkle that touches Katharina immediately. Although she feels feverish and miserable, she takes a close look at the famous painter. He has dense brown hair laced with gray. Atop the prominent forehead a few strands are cut short; otherwise his hair falls well past his ears. A full beard on chin and cheek as well as strong, dark eyebrows underline the vitality of his appearance.

How Katharina envies Cranach's wife, who moves calmly and surely through the room attending to her guests. Barbara Cranach may be about thirty-five. She is large and her figure ample. Maybe even pregnant? In any case, she is wearing the most lavish and beautiful dress Katharina has yet seen. It is dark blue. On the sleeves and at the hem it has white lace. This dress is calf-length, short enough to reveal a chemise of finest dark blue fabric embroidered with dark stars. A beautiful woman in a beautiful home. A husband who puts his hands on her shoulders and includes her in the conversation.

✦   ✦   ✦

Katharina is hot with envy and cold with rage. Look at herself in contrast with this woman. Spat on by the vulgar crowd, no family, no home, not a penny to her name. It gives her no comfort that the other girls have it just as bad. Every one of them begged her parents, in person or in letters, for Christ's sake to get them out of the cloister. And if that wasn't possible, at least to send them money and clothing. Not one of the families did so. Katharina had the least hope of them all. Her father is dead. At home, her stepmother is scarcely able to provide for herself and her sons

(Katharina's stepbrothers Hans, Klemens, and Florian).

Again and again, Katharina arrives at the same self-destructive assessment of her situation: What am I? A runaway nun (which for many people is the same thing as a whore), a noblewoman without property, and already twenty-four years old besides. The Devil himself has his eye on this one! Katharina would like to tear out every bit of her hair, stamp her feet, take the beautiful dishes, the Bohemian glasses, and sweep them off the table—let the Devil take the cloister, Wittenberg, the whole world. She, Katharina, will ride to Hell with him and rage against all those who have brought her to this pass.

First she will set the demons loose on her father. Oh, you hard, stone-faced father. How unbelievably you treated your daughter. How could you throw away your own flesh and blood like that, hand her over to cloister life? Yes, if it were still the way it once was, when they raised a girl lovingly in a cloister until a good man took her in marriage, yes, then I would have understood your putting me into a cloister. But there was none of that. You placed my defenseless youth in chains. Tell me, did you do it for honor's sake? For your honor or mine? It would have been a greater honor for me if you had given me a husband, even if he had been a simple workman. But you didn't want to be seen as stooping so low, no! Oh, how stupid you are. Don't you realize that by putting me into a cloister you really showed people how poor you are?

You didn't want me marrying into poverty, go ahead and say it. You thought that your child with all her desires would break out and cover herself with shame and sin by compromising herself with a stall boy or a cowherd. Yes, if it had only happened that way. But now something far worse has happened . . . And tell me, Father, who should I turn to with my troubles? Do I dare trust my father confessor?

Will you answer to God, Father, for my breaking my vow? Tell God your daughter is not made of wood or iron. Tell him I was tired of the endless masses and psalms, tired of confessing, singing, and chastising. Tell him I will go to mass when I have a longing for God. I will sing when my heart rises up to God. And I've had enough of welts on my back, too.

Don't you know, Father, how much hostility there is behind cloister walls, how much spying and persecution and betrayal? I don't know what you know. But one thing I do know, Father: If I knew for sure you were in Hell (and I'll bet you are), if I knew for sure, and I could pray you out of there with one Hail Mary, Father, I would pray you in deeper instead, because you got me into this miserable situation.

✦   ✦   ✦

"In the name of Christ, maiden, you're ill!" Barbara Cranach has come to Katharina's side, taken her wrist. "She has a high fever. She must lie down. Call Dr. Schurf!"

Katharina knows that the fever in her soul, the heat that comes from hatred, is far more dangerous than the fever of illness—and, above all, far more shameful. She is capable of pursuing her hate-filled thoughts and working herself into such a state that she will pass out. She has known this since her ninth birthday.

It is January 29, 1508. Katharina is still living in the cloister at Brehna. After the None, the nine-year-old girl is summoned by the abbess. Katharina sees the Reverend Mother for the first time in her private rooms. She is sitting at a table vise in which a little wooden figure is secured. The Domina has already chiseled a face out of the wood, and now she is working on shaping the folds of its garment. She turns to Katharina with her distant, friendly smile. "Listen, my child, your parents and I have decided that you will be taken tomorrow morning to Cloister Marienthron in Nimbschen."

Katharina has but one thought, one question: "And Clara?"

The abbess raises her eyebrows. "Clara? Clara Preusser stays here. Dr. Johann Preusser has just commissioned another panel depicting our Lord's Passion."

The Reverend Mother seems to be saying this more to herself. She returns to her carving and explains to Katharina: "A Higher Being guides our footsteps. Everything comes from God."

God. Clara, Clara, God. Why? Why? Why? Katharina doesn't understand, she doesn't want to understand anything anymore—not the Reverend Mother, not God. All she knows is Clara, her only friend in Brehna, is being taken away from her! Katharina doesn't want to hear any more, see any more, feel any more. She screams, pounds her head against the wall, throws herself onto the floor and shrieks.

Sisters come, lift Katharina off the floor, race with her to the column of miracles. (Almost every cloister possesses such a curative site.) Here some of the cloister's precious relics are stored: splinters from Christ's cross and from his crown of thorns. A scrap from the veil that wiped sweat from the Savior's brow. Hair of the Holy Virgin. Remnants of her veil. The shrine has often worked miracles. Made the sick well. A peasant woman, who in anger wished her seven-year-old son to the Devil, hurries with the boy, who is unable to stand, howling and frothing amid convulsions, to this place. Another child, horribly twisted and contorted, is unable to say anything but "Devil." And he is healed. Adults, too, who have fallen under a magic spell are brought here.

Now it is all the sister sacristan can do to carry the screaming Katharina three times around the column. But her faith, and the anxious prayers of the sisters that accompany her every step, give her strength. On the second trip around the column, Katharina has already quieted down, and after the third she lies exhausted in the sacristan's arms. "You, O God, do we praise. You, O Lord, do we exalt." The nuns sing this in happy triumph.

✦   ✦   ✦

It has snowed. Everything is white, so white. Cloister Marienthron rises like a fortress above the quiet and hilly countryside. The road that leads south from the city of Grimma soon makes a steep descent into rolling meadows. Forested hills to the west and the quietly flowing river to the east enclose the meadows and fields that provide the cloister with such rich bounty.

Now the wagon with Katharina has arrived at the cloister estate with its huge orchards. Sister Benedikta is just now telling Katharina that the abbess of Marienthron, the Reverend Mother Margarete von Haubitz, is a blood relative of her, Katharina's, mother. That is why she is taking you in at Marienthron. Out of kindness and compassion, and for your mother's sake.

Kindness and compassion. Katharina hears that often. Gratitude. You lack the gift of gratitude. Katharina is also stigmatized as the one who has occasional bouts of possession by the Devil. The sisters, who tyrannize the young novices more or less, each according to her own character and temperament—though they dominate them absolutely in every case—almost without exception these sisters soon regard their new pupil with a certain respect mixed with repugnance. Katharina realized quickly that a particular reputation preceded her from the cloister in Brehna. She realizes as well that she makes the canonesses (including the Reverend Mother) uncomfortable. Instinctively she has done everything she could to live up to this role again and again.

It was not hard at all for her to respond to prohibitions (which she considered basically unfair) by invoking the Devil. Nor did she have any difficulty attracting attention with conspicuous displays of utter rapture during the liturgy. She hadn't the slightest compunction about telling the other girls of the figures of light that visited her cell at night. Or she would tell them about the Devil, who kept threatening to possess her. Katharina made the frightened girls take an oath of strictest secrecy. This was the only way to be sure that all the canonesses would hear the stories.

Only Ave, who at first listened fearfully along with the others, was let in on her secret. Katharina suggested that Ave join in with these stories. Under no circumstances would Ave do that. She admired Katharina's sang-froid. And she had also quickly seen that because of this behavior Katharina was not so completely at the mercy of the godlike authorities that ruled the cloister. As a friend of the Devil child (as some of the nuns called Katharina), she, Ave, is also shunned.

Cloister Marienthron is organized along strictly hierarchical lines. Absolute queen by the grace of God is the abbess, the Reverend Mother. She is sent by Christ and called to stand at the head of the convent. She governs the cloister and has all attendant rights and duties. For all members of the cloister she is both mother and mistress. As bride of Christ she wears the ring, symbol of her devotion; as one of divine vocation she holds the staff, symbol of her office; as one who has surrendered herself to God she is adorned with the cross, symbolizing the strength of her faith and her willingness to endure suffering.

At the side of the Reverend Mother stands the prioress. She is to counsel the abbess and the convent, and she is responsible for discipline on the premises. The subprioress serves as needed in her place, and the novice mistress attends to the comportment of the young novices. The bursar handles the finances of the cloister, while the cellarer oversees the grain bins; it is she who does business with the peasants. The sacred vestments and vessels are in the care of the sacristan. The sacred music is the province of the choir regent and the cantor. The vestiarian procures clothing for the nuns, the kitchen mistress manages the table, the refectory mistress keeps order in the refectory. The gardener raises vegetables and fruit, and the wine cellarer presses the wine used at mass.

Not only for the young novices, but for the people who live in the vicinity of the cloister as well, Marienthron is the absolute authority. People who hope for God's blessing and above all forgiveness of their sins make pilgrimages here. Cloister Marienthron has many holy sites. The twelve altars of the cloister church are rich in precious relics. In ornate golden capsules and shrines there are bits of wood from the manger in Bethlehem, from Christ's cross and from the cross of one of the thieves, particles from Jesus's crown of thorns, parts of the column they tied him to, a splinter from the table of the Last Supper, a bit of the veil used to wipe the Lord's brow, scraps of fabric from the raiment of the Holy Virgin, from the dress of Maria Magdalena, from the cowl of St. Bernard, the great renewer of the Cistercian order. Virtually endless is the list of other saints whose intercession the cloister has secured by acquiring bits of their mortal remains—a collarbone, for example, or a tooth. Cloister Marienthron owns a total of 367 relics.

The people of the surrounding lands make pilgrimages here. To make it even more worth their while, the cloister has purchased a wealth of indulgences. All who make the pilgrimage to Marienthron at Christmas, Easter, or Pentecost, all who get down on their knees and pray, take part in rogations in the cloister courtyard or in the cemetery, can receive forty days' indulgence for grave transgressions. For lesser sins a year's indulgence. The greatest indulgences are handed out when the cloister celebrates its own consecration day. So the people call this day *Aplas* (from *Ablass*, the German word for indulgence). Then a big fair is held and there are ample profits for the cloister.

Katharina stares at the relics in their shrines, no less fascinated than the pilgrims. Her youthful imagination lends these fragments wings that carry her to places of her desire: to the manger in Bethlehem, where she gazes at the Christ Child and gently strokes his hair. To Christ's cross, where she sheds bitter tears with her suffering Lord. With a shudder, she feels the crown of thorns digging into her own scalp. And the Savior's sweat cloth. How gladly would Katharina have, like Veronica, given him the cool, soft cloth that absorbed the sweat of his pain. Fine as a spider's web, the veil of the sweet Virgin Mary. Golden her hair. Surely God chose her because she is so unearthly sweet and beautiful.

Jesus Christ and the Mother of God. They are close by for Katharina. As long as she has lived at Cloister Marienthron, she has had a clear image of the Mother of God. At the end of the long cloister passage, where it turns toward the chapter room and the refectory, stands a sculpture of the Madonna with the baby Jesus. Mary has long hair parted in the middle, her face is cheerful and full of compassion. And the baby Jesus is tugging merrily at his mother's hair. An image of happy love. And the crucifix that hangs in the window niche of the chapter room defines her image of Christ. That one and no other. Even though there are many Madonnas and many crucifixes in

Marienthron. The Madonna in glory, for example, that hangs at the altar of the cloister church. Or the peasant Madonna, holding a tiny but full-grown Christ in her arms. She has a reproachful look, and rightly so. Also the St. Anne with Mary and the child Jesus, St. Simeon with the boy Jesus, a stone pietà, the huge Last Supper group in the portal chapel—all these figures remain in the background.

On winter evenings, as Katharina hurries along the dark cloister passageways, the cheerful Mary is with her. Or even when in midwinter she gets locked into the old refectory. That is not a rare occurrence. This enormous hall with its massive groin vaults cannot be used in winter because it has no stove. Just a little daylight passes through three deeply recessed windows, and only until afternoon. Little enough. Katharina finds herself here often. For laughing when it is not permitted. For breaking the rule of silence. For forbidden looks. For pretended illness. For tardiness. There have been more than enough grounds for punishment. Every day at the cloister holds many traps. All novices and pupils fear the abandoned refectory. Most of all in the evening, when it is pitch dark and the evil ones come wafting in. Then even screaming doesn't help.

No one can hear it through the thick walls. No one wants to hear, either. Then the horror comes creeping out of the recesses and the vaulting. Then the evil angels lie in wait to lead the sinful child completely astray. Witches—oh yes, even little girls are witches, they ride on their broomsticks through the air. Apostate monks straddle their walking sticks, ghastly dogs lick at you with long tongues, poisonous vipers slither closer to strangle you.

When the terror becomes too great, only one thing helps. Clara Preusser, Katharina's only friend from Brehna, showed it to her. You have to put your hand, if possible holding a crumpled ball of soft fabric, where you are strictly forbidden to put it. Then you have to press gently and slide back and forth, beating a rhythm with your head, faster, harder, everything should be all tense, until it gets warm, even hot, and all sweet at the end. Then comes a kind of paralysis, and complete indifference to all terrors. Then comes sleep. It may take a while, but it does come, for sure.

Katharina learned quickly. It was necessary. Once she doesn't notice in time that the novice mistress is silently opening the door to announce the end of her confinement. For Katharina, the mistress's lament is worse than the blows on her bare back. Worse than being locked up again, this time on a strict fast. (When Katharina has grown up, this recollection overtakes her sometimes without warning. And every time—she has no control over it—every time Katharina lets out a groan of shame.) Katharina never wants to be a child again. Not even on her worst days does she wish she could return to her childhood.

✦ ✦ ✦

Wittenberg, April 12, 1523
It is nine o'clock in the morning. Katharina's sixth day in the world. Two days ago she awoke from her feverish dreams. Barbara Cranach had a chicken broth cooked for her and wheat porridge with butter, cream, and cinnamon.

Katharina recovers quickly. Her first question concerns the other girls. "Ave. Where is Ave?"

Barbara reports that two days ago Ave began working in the apothecary that is part of the house. "She has a good hand for it."

Katharina is not surprised. After all, Ave had lots of practice at the cloister. Together with Dr. Hochholzner, she set up a bloodletting room and prepared potions and ointments. The cloister. It's catching up with her yet again.

"While I was ill, did the Domina—?"

"No, no," comes Barbara's soothing reply to her anxious question. "No, Katharina, there's not been a sound from the cloister."

Now Katharina is utterly certain that the Domina is on their side. That she might even have known about their plans to run away.

Oh, Reverend Mother.

Barbara shows Katharina a broadsheet. It is an open letter that Luther wrote to Leonhard Koppe to show support for his help in the nuns' escape:

> Why nuns can leave the cloister with God's blessing:
> It is a new work that we are beginning. The land
> and the people should be told of it. And if someone
> speaks evil of Councillor Leonhard Koppe and calls
> him a robber (or a fool who allows himself to be
> snared by the damned heretic monk in Wittenberg),
> then I, Luther, call him a blessed robber. We say this
> aloud because we find that this abduction pleases
> God, and on that account it need not fear the light

of day. We also say it so that the honor of the maidens and their relatives not be defamed. There are those who claim that the maidens had allowed themselves to be abducted by young men of loose morals. In fact, Leonhard Koppe and his people led them out of the cloister with all due discipline and respect. We know that many parents would prefer to fetch their children home from cloisters. They know that only man's work is done there, and that the Word of God is not preached to them pure and clear. But—are they allowed to break their vows? That question is asked by some. And—one should not make trouble, say others. To them I say: God wants no vows that are unchristian and harmful. Trouble is only trouble. Necessity breaks iron and asks not about trouble. And so I take responsibility, I who advised that it be done. I take responsibility for Leonhard Koppe and his people, who carried it out. And for the maidens who were in need of rescue. But also for all those who will follow their example. I am utterly sure that we all will be able to stand blameless before God and the world.

At the conclusion of the open letter stand the names of the nine:

Magdalene von Staupitz—Else von Canitz—Veronika and Margarete von Zeschau—Ave and Margarete von Schönfeld—Katharina von Bora—Ave Grosse—Laneta von Gohlis

✦   ✦   ✦

Katharina learns that Luther has been active on their behalf in other ways as well. He has written to Spalatin, court chaplain to Elector Friedrich of Saxony, that he might ask at court for money and clothing for the girls. Also Nikolaus von Amsdorf, professor of theology at Wittenberg and Luther's friend, wrote to Spalatin: "I feel sorry for the girls, they have neither shoes nor clothing."

That is true. As Katharina enters the living room, gently supported by Barbara, her companions are still sitting in their habits. But the mood is confident. The duke has announced that he is having cloth and fine leather sent for the fräuleins. They are all competent seamstresses, except Ave and Katharina, and the two of them have acquired great skill at painting on fine fabrics.

"Now all we have to do is fertilize our hair with a little manure," says Ave von Schönfeld.

"And then we'll go to market and buy ourselves husbands," Veronika announces.

"Sure. Do you have any money?"

No. None of them does. But thanks to Luther's efforts, most of the girls have made contact with friends or relatives who will take them in.

Magdalene von Staupitz, gentle, quiet, smart Magdalene, has the most offers. She is the sister of Vicar General Johann von Staupitz. His name carries weight in Wittenberg.

✦   ✦   ✦

Every time Staupitz visited his sister in the cloister, Katharina used to flood Magdalene with questions. Who knows Luther as well as Johann von Staupitz? Magdalene's reports show Katharina the young Luther as a schoolboy in Magdeburg, fascinated to see the emaciated figure of the prince of Anhalt, who is living as a mendicant friar, carrying a beggar's sack on his back through the streets.

Katharina hears of how, in the years between 1502 and 1505, Luther passes his examinations at the Faculty of Arts. His father no longer addresses him with the familiar *du*, but with the respectful *Ihr.* That does the son good. Luther chooses to sit in on lectures about the classics. Virgil and Plautus accompany him right into the cloister. But that comes later.

In the summer semester of 1505, Luther starts his studies in law. Then they are abruptly broken off.

Luther has visited his parents. On the way back from Mansfeld to Erfurt, he finds himself in a fierce storm. A thunderstorm like the apocalypse. Luther is alone in the sulfurous yellow light. Close by, a bolt of lightning strikes, hurling him to the ground. Katharina, who herself endures mortal fear in thunderstorms, can well understand that a terrified Luther called on Anne, patron saint of miners, and swore to devote the rest of his life to God.

Katharina discovers that there are more events that leave the young student desperately searching for solid ground to stand on. Once—again during a journey—he injures himself in the thigh with the point of his dagger so severely that he is in danger of bleeding to death. Then the plague rages through Erfurt in 1505 and snatches two of his dear friends, both fellow students. Two professors of jurisprudence die, one after the other. Both are a little less than thirty years old.

So much proximity to death. Katharina is familiar with these days and nights full of fear. During her time at Nimbschen she twice saw the plague hold the cloister in its talons. The epidemic raged among the nuns. The death bell rang for days at a time. "Despair makes the monk," or so they say. "Despair makes the nun." Widows knocked at the cloister gate, mothers weeping for their children. They sought the protection of God, who was all they had left.

Katharina can easily imagine the young Luther walking through the streets of Erfurt. Later he will tell Staupitz, "When I was a young magister, I was always sad under the weight of sad events. Thus did I devote much time to reading the Bible."

This, too, Katharina can readily understand. Her life in the cloister is a constant back-and-forth between intense devotion and equally intense revulsion, and while struggling to keep her balance, she has often fallen into bouts of deep depression and thoughts of ending her life. In such times, she, Katharina, clung to Ave or Laneta. But whom did Luther have?

Katharina knows that Luther, too, subscribes to the popular expression: The surest way to Heaven and to God leads through the cloister. Later, Luther will say, "For my salvation I took the vows."

This decision alienates him once again from his father, whom he has tried to please in all things. Hans Luther returns to using *du* with his son. His mother, too, turns away from him. "Have you never heard 'Honor thy father and thy mother'?"

In spite of all this, he enters the cloister on July 17, 1505.

Katharina can practically hear Luther as a novice greedily taking in the words: "If you adhere to the rule, I promise you eternal life." Eternal life. Everything revolves around that. In the cloister of the Augustinians at Erfurt and in the Marienthron cloister of the Cistercians at Nimbschen. That's what they all want, the men and women who consecrate their lives to God: eternal life—or at least not eternal damnation.

Katharina once believed that she would never leave the cloister. Luther believed he wouldn't either: "I was dead to the world. Until God thought it was time."

So Katharina comprehends that at the outset Luther was fighting only one battle: to win God's favor. Luther wishes desperately for God to love him. For him to be on his, Luther's, side. Luther wants God to be God and man, man. And for God to let man stand in his presence.

Oh, Katharina understands well where Luther found his death-defying courage and his strength. No human being can experience spiritual downfall as radically as someone in a cloister who is fighting to win God's favor. To be sure, there are moments of blissful brilliance, in which God and the Truth seem close at hand. But there are more hours of darkest despair.

Keeping vigils, praying, reading, fasting, mortifying the flesh, confessing, celebrating masses to the point of exhaustion, to the point of utter emptiness. Fears of demons torment the taut nerves. Katharina finds out that Luther was so overwrought that he would jump when a leaf fell to the ground.

For Katharina, there were times when she could no longer stand even to hear the name of God or Jesus Christ. When she could not bear the sight of the crucifix. When she felt like running out of Lauds, Prime, Terce, Sext, and None. When, like Luther, she thought, "You are not God, you are the Devil himself! I wish there were no God!"

A life without God—would there then be no fear, no anxiety, no bitter despair, no melancholy? Katharina doesn't know the answer. But it is clear to her that Luther reveals himself to his vicar general, Staupitz, in all his self-torment and doubt. Staupitz tries to help him emerge from his despair. He scolds Luther: fiddlesticks works and poppycock sins!

In 1512 Luther is sworn in as Doctor of the Holy Scriptures, as he says: "I, Doctor Martinus, am called and compelled, I had to become Doctor, without my thanks, purely out of obedience, I had to take the position of Doctor, to swear and affirm on the Holy Scriptures I so love, to preach and teach them pure and true. In the process of this teaching, the papacy has fallen away from me."

Katharina knows that Luther has already been in Rome. That the Holy City disappointed him. Priests read the mass as if it were a circus act. Before Luther gets to the Gospel reading, the priest beside him has already finished the mass. *"Passa, passa, passa,"* he shouts at Luther. "Keep it moving! Come on, let's go!" The Pope does not see Luther.

Staupitz makes Luther professor at the University of Wittenberg. But he also does much more for him. He shows Luther the crucified Christ, reminds him that God loves humankind. Staupitz points the way for Luther out of his anxieties and toward the Gospel.

At that point Katharina doesn't yet know that Luther will help her to reach Wittenberg as well. That the two of them will go on living there until the end of their lives.

✦   ✦   ✦

April 16, 1523

The sun sends streams of brightly colored light through the crown glass windows of Cranach's studio. Two of the painter's journeyman assistants prepare the printing plate for an etching depicting Luther's head. They labor intently with the single lip cutter. Once more, Cranach holds up the pencil drawing on which the printing plate will be based, and compares it with another drawing that shows Luther sporting a mustache and bearded cheeks.

"Is that Luther, too?" asks Katharina. She has come to bring the painter and his journeymen a pitcher of beer.

"Yes," says Cranach, "that is our Luther last year, when he was at the Wartburg disguised as Junker Jörg and had to fear for his life."

Katharina looks at the picture. She hasn't yet seen Luther in person. He did pay a visit to his young protégées, but she was still in bed with her fever. Now she picks up the two drawings: so that's Martin Luther. Katharina already has so many images of Luther in her mind that these two drawings confuse her. Plentiful dark hair surrounds Luther's head in tight curls. Dark eyes rather close together, an almost delicate mouth. Luther looks like a knight or a city councillor—but not like a monk.

"He doesn't look like a monk." She says it aloud.

Cranach laughs. "Indeed he is no shaven-headed cleric. He's a professor, and what a professor!"

The journeyman eyes Katharina and instructs: "Luther is our national hero. And the hero of Wittenberg."

Katharina knows that. All the more credit is due to Luther, then, for making the concerns of so many monks and nuns his own. Now nuns are fleeing their cloisters everywhere. From Beutitz near Weissenfels, from Wiederstedt outside Mansfeld, all around the country the exodus is beginning. Heinrich Kelner of Mittweida, who abducted a nun from the cloister at Sornzig, is beheaded in Dresden. His body is impaled disgracefully on a stake. In spite of this, more and more maidens are running away from Sornzig, although Duke Georg von Sachsen rants and rages against it.

"The contagion is simply stronger than the deterrent," says Cranach when word of the beheading reaches the painter's house.

And Luther helps where he can. In spite of his poverty. His salary is small, he earns only nine gulden, but he gives what he can.

Katharina and the other girls wish to burden him no longer. They work in the house and above all in the Cranachs' large garden. In any case, they don't dare go out. The crude remarks at their arrival cut deep. Besides, they are ashamed of their appearance.

✦ ✦ ✦

On Sunday, toward the eleventh hour, the city councillors of Wittenberg come to call on the girls. Among them are Magister Philipp Reichenbach, Johann Hohndorf, Hieronymus Krapp and Benedikt Pauli. They are wearing caps and rich, flowing shirts beneath fur-trimmed cloaks. Hohndorf, the youngest and liveliest one, calls out to Cranach, who has come out to greet them, "Did you know, our castle provost is planning to take one of the Falk girls as his bride."

"Our Justus Jonas, really?" Barbara Cranach wants to know which of the noble Erich Falk's daughters it is.

"Katharina, I think."

Magister Reichenbach, a still youngish man with a head of blond curls and a long, pointed nose, reports with a sidelong glance in the direction of the escaped nuns, "One barefooted monk is now a shoemaker. He took the blacksmith's daughter. Another has become a baker and has married as well. One Augustinian is now a cabinetmaker, and he too has taken a wife."

Pauli blows his nose forcefully. "Yes, it's like that everywhere. Monks and priests are letting their tonsures grow out and taking wives."

Krapp says jokingly, "And it seems the church's women don't want to be left behind, either."

Katharina feels the blood rising to her temples. She tries to control herself, but her voice comes out higher and louder than she intends: "I call upon God and my own conscience as my witnesses that it was not impulse or desire that drove us from the cloister—as the people here are shouting in the streets. They say we were running away from our orders because we were tired of the cloister's stillness. So that we might live in the freedom of the flesh and give vent to our worldly desires. Oh no, it is not like that! We have honorable and grave complaints. Our conscience has infallible imperatives based on God's Word. So we will allow no one to accuse us of frivolity, wantonness, or any other improper intentions. And we certainly did not go running off because of any men."

"Now, now, now Miss Katharin," Cranach tries to calm Katharina, who has talked herself into a fury. The councillors are taken aback, they stare at Katharina. And she goes on, although quieter now, "No, it is like this: In the last few years the writings of Martin Luther have come to us in the cloister. Even before they were forbidden by religious and secular authorities. At first, these teachings struck us as exceedingly strange and disconcerting. There was much in them that contradicted the laws and orders we had been taught.

"But then we began in all secrecy to discuss and dispute amongst ourselves. And we sensed, deep within our souls, that in Martin Luther's teachings the Holy Scriptures speak with their brightest and clearest voice. Suddenly, we all had an urgent desire to read these writings again and again. And the more we did, the more we understood how magnificently this highly learned, enlightened man has worked with the Holy Scriptures. How his approach to them is entirely pure and clean. How he illuminates and clarifies obscure texts by drawing on other verses that are more readily understood. We realized that Luther possesses the greatest of mastery in working with Scripture. That we women of the cloth, with our instruction in Latin and in the Scriptures, that we too can readily understand all of it. We were soon convinced that the new teachings stand on a foundation that is true, strong, and thoroughly Christian.

"That is how we came to love Luther's teachings. And with immense gratitude we saw that God, in his great, fatherly mercy, took pity on us in our misery. He saw us stumbling about in our hunger and thirst for the truth. And now he has given us the living water of pure, divine teachings."

The girls look at Katharina with admiration, and a little embarrassment. Only Ave says with shining eyes, "Yes, just as Katharina says, that's how it is."

The councillors turn away in silence. They look at each other with brows furrowed.

Then they face each other, so that they almost form a circle, and speak among themselves concerning official business. "The council of Wittenberg has told the bare-footed monks and the Augustinians to clear out of the cloisters. And all the prostitutes are expelled from the city. If a man is living in adultery, he must either marry the woman or stay away from her. The council has assigned fourteen men to tell the poor that they should stop giving alms to monks. The council gives to each according to his need. To an old priest six gulden, but a young one should learn a trade."

The girls get the point. The official visit has ended. Barbara Cranach escorts them out.

"Did you learn at the cloister to be such a good

impromptu speaker?" she asks Katharina with half a smile.

The girls say nothing. Katharina, too, is silent. She senses that her behavior was inappropriate. But she does not understand why. She only knows that she has displeased the Cranachs, these people who have treated her so generously. (She has put off the others, too, of course, but that's not as important to her.) Sadly, she says to Barbara, "I promised the cook I'd bake some fine butter rolls for the noonday meal."

"You go right ahead. So they'll turn out as tasty as those raisin cakes were yesterday." As she speaks, Barbara flashes Katharina a quick smile.

The Cranach kitchen is somewhat similar to the cloister kitchen at Marienthron. Only not as large. Here, too, a mighty stove stands at the center. In the chimney corner is an earthen oven for baking bread. On shelves along the walls an abundance of dishes. Ceramic bowls, pitchers with spouts and handles. Roasting pans in all imaginable sizes, large dough baskets, mortars, pestles. Anna, the cook, works with four kitchen maids and a boy who tends the ovens and shreds cabbage. The girls are pounding boiled chicken in a mortar and then passing it through a sieve to make a creamy soup. Proudly, the cook shows Katharina a bowl of olives. For a spice cake, almonds are being shelled, dates and figs chopped fine. Something in Katharina keeps her from revealing how familiar this all is from her days in the cloister kitchen. They ate well at Marienthron. Katharina can prepare stuffed pastries, either sweet or with vegetables, just as expertly as she dresses and roasts meat. She knows how to make good use of expensive spices like cinnamon and cloves, dried currants, anise or ginger. The same goes for apples, onions, or honey. She knows how to prepare exquisite fish dishes and, yes, even how to brew beer.

Katharina shows the cook how she must chop up the butter quickly and knead it right away into the thrice-sifted flour. The cook watches with respect how adroitly Katharina works.

And in the meantime she reports to this noble cloister maiden, who doesn't yet dare attend church, how much things have changed these days. "The parish church is closed now on weekdays. There's just a mass on Sundays. It's in German, and somebody preaches. Today it was Dr. Luther again. He doesn't wear a cassock anymore, just a black robe and a biretta with the edges turned up. First he had us sing psalms. Then he read the Gospel. Then he preached about faith and about Hell, but I fell asleep. And just as I woke up, he was blessing wine in two big cups and giving it to the communicants to drink. When it was gone, he blessed some more. And he said you didn't have to go to confession, and you could take communion even if you had already eaten. He said what was important was strong faith and not an empty stomach. But there were some, too, that went up for communion who had spent the night before drinking and carousing. I saw them."

The other maids prick up their ears. One sets the salt pestle back into the mortar and remarks that now all the old ways are under attack. "One old woman went into the castle church and stuck her potherbs into the holy-water font. She got them good and wet. Then students came into the church, and they tried to take her herbs away. Well, the old woman shook those wet herbs and spattered the students right in the eyes. Then one of them ran up to her, grabbed her, and pulled her clothes up behind until she was uncovered. Then he sat her down, bare-bottomed, into the holy water. Everyone who saw it laughed."

Everyone in the kitchen laughs, too. Katharina wipes flour from her hands. She goes down to the apothecary to see Ave. The workroom is filled with potent smells from the fresh and dried herbs in earthen vessels. Ave is crushing senna leaves in a pestle, pulverizing poppies, arnica, and orchids.

The head of the Cranach apothecary is Basilius Axt, a young doctor of medicine. Lucas Cranach has begun teasing Ave, saying that Axt is so in love he can't tell the sage from his thimble. He'll end up in prison yet, says Cranach.

Katharina is not surprised that Ave is much sought after. She herself has fought for the girl's love. Katharina will never forget the day Ave first arrived at the cloister.

✦　✦　✦

Holy Saturday, 1514
Early in the afternoon, during the None, Katharina has suddenly felt nauseated and dizzy. She remembers with a sigh that her menses are due. She is allowed to return to her cell and lie down. Katharina is freezing, as she is so often. Her legs are ice cold. As she stretches them, she gets a cramp in one calf. A pain whose senselessness always makes her furious.

"That's the punishment for your arrogance." Adelheid, the novice mistress, says this.

Juta, who tends the sick, had advised Katharina to brace her feet immediately against the cold floor.

"Damn. Jesus, forgive me." Katharina doesn't know why the curses always come to her more readily than the Psalms.

"Humbly I pray to you, concealed Godhead." Katharina wants to be humble. And obedient. And faithful before God. She can't do it. She can't do anything. The number of her sins grows from day to day. Often she falls asleep during the prayers. She shows no regret. Talks back. Blows with a stick and a diet of just bread and water make her defiant, but also miserable.

Katharina has the same dream again and again. She is sitting on a very small island, scarcely two yards square, and this island lies in a vast sea. The waves grow high, the island begins to totter. Far off on the horizon, Katharina sees the outline of a castle. She has a sweet, painful yearning to live there. Yet she knows she will never be able to reach this castle. Katharina looks up at the sky, and there she sees, surrounded by a radiant halo, the Mother Abbess on a golden throne. The canonesses seated to either side form a golden choir. The Domina calls:

"Listen, daughter, and look, and incline your ear . . ." And the voice of the Domina becomes a muffled din. The sea rolls and roars. Now Katharina can only see the Domina and the canonesses, she can't hear any of what they are saying to her. The Mother Abbess is far, far off. Out of reach. Katharina clings to the tottering island. She knows that she is dreaming, but she wants to wake up.

Dreams. They are a window onto the Beyond, says Sister Mechthildis. Her mind is confused, the others say. Sister

Mechthildis is old, unbelievably old. Over eighty. On cold days she sits in the infirmary, rosary in her hands. Her pale, red-rimmed eyes seem to take in everything. In the summer she wanders about the little garden inside the cloister. She'll stand motionless for a long time looking at the sundial painted onto the south wall of the cloister building. Or she'll tear leaves or flowers from the bushes and put them onto her hair, and then sometimes she'll laugh and dance. Then the sisters come and gently lead her inside. There is a secret about Mechthildis. Once she was a prioress, a highly educated woman. She is a descendant of the house of the Saxon prince elector. The Cloister Marienthron is indebted to her, who wrote both Latin and German, for all of its psalters and breviaries.

Mechthildis used to take illegible or incomprehensible passages in old books and (mainly because there was often a shortage of paper), carefully wash them clean and redo the lettering. She mastered the art of repairing holes in old parchment using colored silk. Despite her occasional confusion and her physical decline, Mechthildis is still listened to at Marienthron. The Reverend Mother visits her often. Everyone knows she is devoted to the old prioress with much love and admiration. They say of Mechthildis that she was born the Countess Elisabeth von Meissen-Landsberg and engaged at age fifteen to the young Duke Boleslaus von Schweidnitz in Silesia. On the day before the wedding, which had been prepared with great pomp, the seventeen-year-old duke was killed in a hunting accident. After that, so they say, the young Countess Elisabeth wouldn't so much as look at another suitor. Since she was unusually beautiful, many tried to win her hand. When her father finally attempted to arrange a marriage against her will, Elisabeth refused, insisting instead that she be allowed to enter a cloister. If it cannot be Boleslaus, she said, then it can only be Jesus Christ. And so the young countess donned the robe at sixteen, and only a year later she took her eternal vow.

The young sisters and the novices are uncomfortable around the old woman. They know Sister Mechthildis has visions. She can predict deaths.

In the winter of 1513, Katharina has fallen gravely ill. She has vomited food and drink. From day to day she grows more miserable. Sister Magdalene, the infirmary mistress, who is also Katharina's aunt, brings her tea and thin gruel. Her stomach can't keep anything down. On the sixth day, the father confessor hears her confession and administers last rites. Katharina believes, along with everyone else in the cloister, that she is going to die. She asks that Sister Mechthildis visit her. The old nun comes. Katharina asks, "Have you seen me with the candle, Mechthildis?"

"No, child. I have seen nothing. And I have kept watch all night . . ."

Then Katharina knows that she is not going to die. For Sister Mechthildis sees every nun who is about to die on the eve of her death, in the dormitory. The dying nun sits outside her cell holding an extinguished candle, a white figure of light that shows itself to Mechthildis alone. Mechthildis has never been mistaken.

Katharina says, "I am afraid of death, Mechthildis."

"You must open your heart to life, child, then death becomes your brother."

"I keep dreaming about my mother, Mechthildis. Will I find her again when I am with God?"

"Trust your dreams, child, in them is hidden the gateway to eternity."

Katharina doesn't understand Mechthildis's words. Still, her heart is comforted.

The gateway to eternity. Katharina looks through the window of her cell. Outside the dormitory is the cloister garden, beyond that lie the fields of the cloister estate. Katharina sees a peasant in the field walking behind the plow. The peasant seems old, Katharina sees his white beard. He is wearing a gray cloak over his blue tunic. With his left hand he holds the stem of the plow, in his right the whip he uses to drive his two oxen. His back is bent. He has to strain to drive the plow deep into the limy soil. Elsewhere, Katharina sees men and women pruning fruit trees and hoeing the earth. Once again she wishes she could fly out her cell window and go soaring over the hilly countryside, far, far away. But . . . where to? Who would take her in? Katharina is filled with longing, and she doesn't know what for. She is unhappy, and she doesn't know why.

From the little rooftop turret, the bell calls. Six in the afternoon. With a sigh, Katharina goes to the new refectory. It is smaller and friendlier than the old one, which is no longer used. On the long tables, the tin plates stand in a perfectly straight row.

There is one cup and one spoon for each diner. On the

wall at the head of the room, for all to see, hangs the crucifix. Katharina squeezes sullenly into her place. The bench is hard. Every time Katharina moves, she feels the blood run out between her legs. Katharina hates her menses—the bloody cloths that are constantly slipping. "The Devil take it. Jesus, you are my life."

The Reverend Mother enters, along with the prioress and the novice mistress. They bring in two girls in worldly clothes. Margarete and Ave von Schönfeld. Ave.

Katharina forgets all her troubles. She sees a slight figure, probably a little younger than herself. A fine, slender neck, dense, dark curls, a pretty nose. Most beautiful are her eyes. Big and blue, framed by dark, unusually thick lashes. Ave looks around, her eyes lively and apparently quite free from timidity or shyness. The novice mistress, Adelheid, directs the two candidates to Katharina's table. She ushers Ave to the place across from Katharina. Katharina gives Adelheid, with whom she is otherwise continually locking horns, the sweetest, most endearing look she can muster. Which throws the novice mistress into utter confusion.

Katharina is delighted. Ave, the new girl, is hungry. Everyone can see that. Her soup disappears fast, and so does the flatbread. Katharina quietly slides her bread across the table. Ave's eyes grow even bluer. They look deep into Katharina's. The older girl's heart rejoices. She knows that she is alone at Marienthron no longer. Later on, her voice is loud and joyful as she prays at Compline:

I will bless the Lord at all times;
    his praise will be ever in my mouth.

I will glory in the Lord;
  let the humble hear and rejoice.
Proclaim with me the greatness of the Lord;
  let us exalt his Name together.
I sought the Lord, and He answered me
  and delivered me out of all my terror.
The angel of the Lord encompasses those who fear him,
  and he will deliver them . . .

Keep us O Lord, as the apple of your eye;
Hide us under the shadow of your wings.

With the *us* Katharina means Ave and herself.

  After Compline the cloister falls quiet, the great silence. The Schönfeld sisters will live in separate cells. Ave moves in with Laneta von Gohlis. Katharina knows she's had enough joy for one day. But she also knows that Ave will share a cell with her. So far, she hasn't the faintest idea how she will make it happen, but she will—no, she must— come up with something. Since Katharina was separated from Clara von Preusser, she has opened her heart to no one. Nor has she wanted to. Today, though, Ave's affection has fallen on her like a ray of sunlight.

  The next morning the death bell tolls. Sister Mecht- hildis has died during the night. Dressed in her white habit, on her head a wreath of rosemary, in her hands the rosary, there she lies in the chapel. Katharina feels sad and remorseful. Why didn't she visit Mechthildis more often? Only now does she realize how much she loves this sister. Prayerfully she joins the others in maintaining the vigil.

Four days and four nights in shifts. Katharina would like to touch the fine, now waxen hands. But she didn't do it in life, so she won't do it now, in death. With an aching heart she prays:

> My soul thirsts for God
> For the living God
> When shall I come
> And behold the face of God?

✦　✦　✦

The Lord has given Katharina Ave, Mechthildis he has taken away. Yes, Katharina knows it now, as tears well up in her throat. She knows that Mechthildis was her friend.

The day of burial is here. Once more, Katharina bids farewell to the waxen doll that Mechthildis now is. Eight canonesses bring the coffin into the church. At nine o'clock Father Abbot Peter von der Pforte conducts the requiem. The sisters carry the coffin, light bearers accompany it, and in a long procession the entire convent follows, praying. Chancel and high altar in the cloister church are draped in black. The great yellow candles at the high altar are decorated with black skulls. At each side of the high tomb, which is surrounded by thirty-six candles on tall candlesticks, stand three boys from the house of the Saxon princes. They carry flaming torches. The coffin of Mechthildis is adorned with a cross and a wreath of flowers. The abbess's staff lies on a black cushion.

The prayers swell and fade. Katharina feels miserable and dizzy. She is staring at the coffin, but she sees Mechthildis sitting outside her cell. As a figure of light holding an extinguished candle.

Many people of the world are in the church. Members of the prince's family. Today, in honor of Mechthildis, poor women are given food and money. For thirty days food will be served in the cloister at Mechthildis's place and then given to the poor.

For the Mother Abbess, Mechthildis's death is a great loss. At the funeral, Katharina sees her face taut with pain. Katharina wants this pain to be of use to her, Katharina. She petitions the Domina for an interview. It is granted for the following morning, following the Sext. Katharina knows that her wish will be fulfilled—either today or never.

✦   ✦   ✦

The Reverend Mother is sitting at her writing table. She smiles as Katharina enters. The abbess draws her eyebrows together in an odd way that turns every smile into a silent question. It is these eyebrows that set her face apart from others. They are thick and dark. Like two clear, strong arches above those intelligent eyes that radiate trustworthiness and warmth. Other than Ave, the Reverend Mother is pretty much the only person whose approval matters to Katharina. At the same time, she is in awe of this woman. It is hard for her to imagine that, outside in the world, the Domina is her aunt.

"You want to speak with me, my child?"

"Oh, Reverend Mother . . ."

Katharina weeps. The Domina looks at her, then asks softly, "Mechthildis?"

Katharina nods silently, although she knows that it's not about Mechthildis, or at least not only about her. She is ashamed because she wants to exploit the Domina's love for Mechthildis, her emotional upset at the death of this motherly friend. Katharina knows how alone the abbess is. How hard she tries, despite all her sternness and discipline, to be fair and just to everyone. Even to Katharina, who is having such a hard time adjusting to the narrow frame of humility, obedience, and renunciation.

Katharina has often witnessed this woman's greatness of heart. When the cloister messenger's wife died, the Domina took in their four-year-old daughter; she also raised the orphan of a laborer who died of the plague. And a foundling left one morning at the gate—the Domina kept her at the cloister as well. She had a poor woman from the village who had a horrible growth on her face taken into the cloister and treated with herbs. To the Schwaigers, whose farm was burning, she sent the father confessor with consecrated objects to cast into the flames. When a dead woman was found in the village and no priest was willing to bury her, the abbess arranged for a burial and had a mass read for the poor woman's soul. Once a man pursued by the authorities pled that she hide him. The Domina had inquiries made at court, whether he might not be pardoned. Her intercession saved his life.

Oh yes, Katharina feels small in the presence of this great woman. Yet even if her wish is selfish, she had to come. In tears, she asks the Domina to let Ave, the new candidate, share a cell with her. For a while the Domina is silent. Then she says, "I will speak with the prioress and the novice mistress." And: "I have always tried to forget that you are the child of my departed sister. You resemble her more and more every day."

The Mother Abbess turns away. Katharina leaves. Her wish will be fulfilled, that much she knows. But the joy she expected to feel is not there.

✦   ✦   ✦

Much time has passed since then. So much time. Now Katharina is out in the world. She is free. Yet her thoughts are constantly at Marienthron. She may have taken off the habit, but that didn't strip away the cloister.

She speaks with Ave and finds she feels the same way. "In order to forget the cloister we'd have to shed our skins," says Ave.

Today, on the twenty-third of April, 1523, the former nuns are going to venture out for the first time with Barbara Cranach into the city and to the market. All the girls are excited. They've never been in a city. While they're getting dressed, Magdalene von Staupitz tells how a nun once got the better of her. "I was six when I arrived at the cloister. Until my tenth year, I did not leave it. I couldn't even go out onto the cloister estate or into the village. One day a big ram got loose and wandered into the cloister garden. I asked a nun who happened by what it was. She said that it was a woman of the world who lived in sin. So the Devil made horns grow on her. She told me this in all sincerity, and I went on believing it for a long time."

Everyone laughs. "In the cloister they also say that

women of the world wear dresses cut out at the neck so you can see almost half their breasts."

"At court they do," says Barbara. She helps Ave sling a fine, blue scarf artfully around her head to form a loose bonnet. The *Schapel*, a wreath of flowers or foliage that young girls like to wear, they decide to save until their hair has grown back. They have all made frequent visits to the Cranach bathing room, where they have washed the matted stubble on their heads with an herbal tonic. Now their hair is slowly recovering from the constant pressure of the veil. It shines, begins to form ringlets, each girl's hair in its own way.

Katharina finds Ave's head of curls the most beautiful; Ave, in turn, admires Katharina's fine but very dense hair, which hugs her head like a dark brown cap. Katharina has made herself a snood of red silk. She attaches it to an embroidered ribbon, and Ave ties it for her at the back of her neck. The girls, just three weeks ago a white flock in rumpled habits and matted stubble heads, have metamorphosed into burgher women and burgher girls. They have patterned their new clothes after Barbara Cranach's dresses. The prince sent them fabric from Flanders and several simple, white chemises. From the fabric they sewed themselves bodices with short sleeves and skirts that gather at the waist with drawstrings.

As the girls leave the courtyard they find themselves already at the market, since the painter's house stands directly on the market square. The weather is typical for April. For a moment the sun comes out, as if by coincidence, only to disappear again behind wind-driven clouds.

To the girls, the city of Wittenberg appears great and mysterious. It harbors some four thousand souls within its walls. Lucas Cranach has told Katharina that the city consists of 387 houses. But building is going on everywhere. Beside the houses, especially near the city gates, ladders stand, wood and loam lie in piles. Ladders and poles impede the progress of peasant carts, hitched to horses or oxen, as they enter the gates.

Despite the still chilly weather, most people are barefoot. Or they are wearing wooden clogs. Small children scuffle, play with hoops and crossbows. Sometimes bare bottoms peek out from under their smocks. Katharina notices that most of the peasants and their wives, walking alongside their carts or donkeys, are gnomishly short, and that they walk with backs bent. They look worn-out, timidly keeping their eyes on the ground before them. Most are also carrying heavy baskets or bundles on long poles. A barefooted peasant woman is on horseback, with one small child clinging to her in the front and another from behind. The peasant carries a long sword, but his linen jacket is patched, and under it his shirt is in tatters.

Barbara Cranach leads her guests to the castle. Wittenberg is the Saxon residence of the Ernestine Prince Friedrich III. The prince has had a completely new castle erected where the castle of the previous rulers, the Askanians, once stood. Barbara tells the girls that her husband and the painter Albrecht Dürer from Nuremberg decorated the magnificent grand halls. Soon thereafter, the prince had the castle church built. The girls want to go inside, but the door is locked. "This is the door where it all began, isn't it?" asks Laneta.

"Yes. This is where Luther nailed up his ninety-five theses." Barbara says it was much more important that he sent them to Archbishop Albrecht of Mainz and to many bishops: after all, Luther did want to debate with them. He implored them to reprimand their lying indulgence preachers, and above all Tetzel. But the man in Mainz didn't answer Luther at all. He passed the whole matter on to Rome.

Barbara stops and stands in front of the girls, recalling vividly, "You should have seen it: within two weeks these theses had reached all Germany, and nearly all of Christendom in four. It was as if the angels themselves were the couriers and they were carrying the word right before everyone's eyes. No one could imagine what talk they caused. The theses were soon translated from Latin into German, and everyone very much liked their message. Everyone except the indulgence preachers and the archbishop and all those who daily enjoy the power of the Pope.

"Everything Martinus writes," Barbara continues after a moment, "everything that comes from him the people want to read. When he debated in Leipzig, right away there were pamphlets reporting about it all over Germany. At the autumn trade fair in Frankfurt, one thousand four hundred copies were sold within a few days."

"Yes," Ave Grosse confirms, "even in the cloister we were getting copies of his pamphlets."

"And how are his writings circulated among the people?" It's Veronika von Zeschau who wants to know. "The people can't even read."

"Whoever can't read just has a student read it to him, or

he goes to a school and has someone explain it to him there. And everyone can buy the pamphlets for very little money. They're for sale everywhere—at the market, outside the church door when mass lets out, even at the city gates. And there are carriers who walk about selling them."

Barbara Cranach is well known throughout the city. Today she attracts even more attention than usual as she and her nine protégées walk from the castle church to the city hall. Here, too, construction is going on. A new city hall is to be built. Everything is covered with scaffolding. Many wealthy burghers and professors are replacing their whitewashed houses with new ones of stone. Handsome burgher houses are taking shape, with broad entryways and ornate gables. But in the alleys there are still many little huts of clay with thatch roofs, looking quite wretched.

Soon, Katharina is feeling overwhelmed. The narrow, dark alleys are something entirely new for her; the market square alone with all its commotion is enough to disorient and tire her. On top of that, she is constantly having to lift the hem of her skirt. As soon as she is in the shadow of a house whose bay window or little tower extends out over the alley, she has to watch that she doesn't step into garbage, wood, stones, or mud. Ugh! A devil of a mess. And just look at her shoes! Suddenly, all the things she has so longed for are just too colorful, too loud. All the people. Bakers, cloth makers, butchers, furriers, smiths, coopers, linen weavers, all running busily and hawking their wares. Interspersed among them, students in brightly colored jerkins and slit trousers. They steal turnips and eggs from the marketwives, or they beg: A penny for a poor student.

For a gulden, Barbara buys a pig for slaughter. The butcher will bring it right to the Cranach kitchen. The other girls are just as disoriented and exhausted as Katharina. They are all happy when the Cranach courtyard gate closes again behind them.

In the great living room sits Luther.

Katharina, who is seeing him for the first time in person, is disconcerted. So that's him! So this man with dark, curly hair, joking and carrying on a lively discussion with Cranach, Johannes Bugenhagen, and Bürgermeister Pauli, is Martin Luther. Now his dark, alert eyes fall on Katharina. He inquires whether she has recovered from her fever. Katharina is about to thank him for his help with their escape when she sees him turn to greet Ave. Later on as well, she sees that Luther pays close attention whenever Ave speaks or is spoken to. Katharina also sees that Luther will keep up his end of the lively conversation, but then lean back and sit very still. He seems exhausted and worried. Katharina almost can't imagine that this average-sized, friendly, young-looking man has lit such a powerful fire in the world. That he forces princes, bishops, kings, emperors, and the Pope to grapple with his doctrines. At this moment it becomes clear to her that Luther could not accomplish all this himself. One man alone is far too weak. Martin Luther must have received the strength he needed from God.

Luther apologizes to the Cranachs and to the girls for staying away so long: "Believe me, for my work I need two scribes and two chancellors. I do almost nothing all day but compose letters. I preach at the cloister, preside at table, supervise students, serve as vicar (which practically means being prior of eleven cloisters), I am controller of our fishponds at Litzkau and attorney on behalf of the Herzberg monks at Torgau, I lecture on Paul at the university and collect material on the psalter." Luther sighs.

The girls convey their gratitude to him. Each tells Luther how her future, her progress in the world has taken shape in the meanwhile.

Magdalene von Staupitz is leaving for Grimma tomorrow. In honor of her dear brother, Dr. Johann Staupitz, and out of gratitude to him, the Augustinian monks of that city have presented her with a house there. Else von Canitz will travel with her. Relatives in Grimma have offered her a home as well. Laneta von Gohlis will go to her sister's home in Colditz. Ave Grosse will join her brothers on their property in Trebsen. Veronika and Margarete are off to the home of their uncle, Wolfgang von Zeschau. Margarete and Ave von Schönfeld will be moving into the home of Magister Reichenbach. Ave will continue to work in the Cranach apothecary.

And Katharina?

"Nobody wants you." Else von Canitz says it softly, but everyone hears her.

Katharina's cheeks are burning. She knows that she is poorer than any peasant out there at the market. Yes, where is she to go? This thought is with her day and night. The cook hinted at it. In the city, the people are all talking about the noble maidens. Above all about Katharina von Bora. Arrogance, they say. Pride and arrogance. None of the wealthy burghers will take Katharina into his home.

In the silence Cranach speaks, as if all had been decided long since. "Well, Katharina von Bora will remain in our house. We simply can't do without her, can we, Barbara?"

Barbara Cranach smiles in agreement.

That is the answer to all Katharina's troubles.

2

LUCAS CRANACH'S HOUSE is the most splendid burgher's house in Wittenberg, and Cranach the wealthiest man. He is the elector's court painter, Wittenberg city councillor and treasurer, apothecary, and wine merchant. Mayor, too, for a time. So many titles. Actually, Cranach spends most of his time painting. Katharina is envious when she sees him sitting in his great studio. He has an embroidered Kirghiz cap on his head; his loose, gray painter's tunic is thoroughly covered with spatters of paint.

Cranach and his helpers produce the paints themselves. Using a grinding wheel on a piece of marble, plant or mineral ingredients are reduced to a fine powder and then moistened with gum arabic. This is necessary so that they will permanently adhere to the vellum or canvas. Katharina can scarcely get her fill of gazing at the colors. Besides black and white there are the precious blue hues. They are made from cobalt ores found in Saxony. Malachite from Hungary for the green; iris leaves, too, are pounded to make green. Cinnabar red comes from quicksilver with sulfur, vermilion from heating white lead. Ocher produces a deeper red. Yellow hues are developed from a compound of sulfur and arsenic. Violet is garnered from garden heliotrope, black from soot or pulverized black stone.

Katharina would dearly love to work in the atelier. But she has other things to do. Barbara, who in addition to her own large household must also tend to the apothecary shop and the wine business, needs Katharina's help, especially now that she is pregnant.

And now Katharina must hurry to the market. In the kitchen they are short of veal bones and spices for the aspic, and that's not all. Barbara also needs needles, yarn, string, and white canvas. Katharina exchanges a hurried greeting with Ave in the apothecary. She is beautiful. Ach, Ave... She is standing with Dr. Axt in front of an anatomical diagram of the head. Katharina has never seen what the inside of a human head looks like. Not much different from the pig and calf heads she is familiar with from the kitchen. Dr. Axt explains that the faculty of visualization, of imagination, resides in the human brain. With their brains, human beings think, recall past events, and are able to see and hear, taste and smell.

Now Dr. Axt unrolls a parchment that shows an entire person. Or rather two. One from the front, one from the back. The one from the front is evidently a boy; anyway, his whole body, including the genital area, is covered by the twelve signs of the zodiac. The picture shows the influence of the constellations on the human body. People are divided into categories. There are four temperaments: sanguine, or full-blooded; phlegmatic, or lymphatic; choleric, or bilious; melancholic, or given to black bile.

Dr. Axt explains that science further distinguishes according to people's disposition toward heat and dryness, and according to the proportion of masculinity and femininity in their character. Further distinctions are made according to their association with the directions of the four winds. Thus are the primary groups arrived at within the zodiac circle: Aries, Leo, and Sagittarius are hot and dry, choleric, masculine, and easterly. Taurus, Virgo, and Capricorn are cold and dry, melancholic, feminine, and westerly. Gemini, Aquarius, and Libra are hot and wet, sanguine, masculine, and southerly. Cancer, Scorpio, and Pisces are cold and wet, phlegmatic, feminine, and northerly. Katharina was born on January 29. So she is an Aquarius.

But what else? What does Katharina know about her body? So far, only that she has her menses every twenty-eight days. She was thirteen when it took her by surprise. What panic she went through! Why is blood coming from there, of all places? When you have a nosebleed, you lie down and it stops. So Katharina lay down, but it didn't stop. And it felt like knives cutting into her belly. Was she sick? Was she going to die? Finally her aunt, the infirmary mistress, came and brought her the belt and the pieces of linen. Showed her how to attach them to the belt. "You aren't a child anymore," said Aunt Lene.

Katharina isn't sure that the deathly fear doesn't haunt her still. In any case, she is frightened anew every month by the blood that flows out of her, often in large quantities.

Unclean blood, they say.

Why unclean? And why does it flow only from women? Besides this annoying function of her body, Katharina scarcely knows anything about herself. Not until she lived in the Cranach house did she see herself naked. There were no mirrors in the cloister. At least not for the nuns. But the Cranachs have a wall mirror from Venice. After her first bath (and often since then) Katharina looked at herself for a long time. Her breasts are high and full; she has a narrow waist and long legs. She is taller than Ave and the other girls—except for Magdalene von Staupitz, who is quite tall and downright spindly. In the cloister it was a sin to look at your body. Because doing so leads to pleasure. And pleasure is a sin.

It was also a sin to lie in your cell at night holding Ave tight in your arms. To lie naked and find comfort in Ave's skin and her warmth. To feel how her nipples stand up, get hard. To laugh about it was a sin, too.

Thou shalt not be unchaste. That'll get you a beating with the switch. On your bare bottom, all over.

Fasting in your cell on only bread and water. That will drive the desires out of you.

Far from it. They'll all go to Purgatory for their unchaste dreams. At least all of those who swore chastity in the cloister. Those in the world God forgives. After all, they have to bear children and worry about money.

Honestly, who can keep that vow? Maybe St. Benedict was able to. In the solitude of the mountains, where silence is an uninterrupted conversation with God. But why did he keep leaving his cloisters? Like Robert of Molesmes and St. Bernard, who set out from their cloisters for the solitude of Cîteaux in order to find their way back to the purity of Benedict's doctrine? Benedict taught poverty, strict simplicity. In life, in the liturgy. He taught love of the incarnate and crucified Lord. He taught the adoration of Mary.

Then why does the father confessor lead Katharina down into the dark vaults where the beer kegs are stored? Why does he stroke her, a girl of only nine, in the places you're not allowed to touch? Why does he give Katharina a honeycomb? And upstairs in the convent, why does he never look at her? Katharina doesn't find his stroking repulsive. But every time he does it, she wishes she were with the others, upstairs. "You must not tell anyone, my child." Katharina knows this anyway. Now will she end up in Hell?

Katharina has never told anyone. Not even Ave. Ave would have asked questions. And Katharina would have had to tell her too much.

Once, they're lying close together (although they were long since forbidden to do so. But all the girls change cells at night. There's a lot of tiptoeing and giggling in the great silence. Sometimes it is found out, then there are beatings and fasting. So what?) as they discuss in whispers their impending flight, and Ave says, "I wonder what it's like to lie naked with a man."

The information they have is fairly limited. Ursula von Wolffen, a widowed noblewoman who recently took her vows, has little good to say about married life. "I'm just glad it's over with."

"Why, why?" the young nuns don't stop asking her.

Ursula tells them: "My husband drank a lot of wine and beer. Then he got rough. He smashed dishes. He hit me. The servants, too. He was always very crude when he slept with me. He also slept with the maid and with the cook.

He said I was a witch who put a hex on her own children."

Ursula's children died while they were still very small. Ursula's drunken husband fell down the stairs.

Ursula is twenty-seven. She wants to stay in the cloister.

From other sisters they hear that in the world there are men who are true devils. Not only do they sleep with their maids, they get their own mothers and sisters pregnant, even their daughters. These monsters are sure of going straight to Hell. But here on earth they are seldom made to suffer for it, because no one accuses them publicly.

Women, by contrast, must be on their guard. If they make a man angry, he can denounce them as witches. And then, may God have mercy.

✦ ✦ ✦

Witch, you witch. That is more than an epithet. It is a death sentence. Well, are there really witches? Katharina, now eighteen, can scarcely believe it. But she learns from the other sisters: The unholy angels, the demons who populate the lower heavens, have supernatural means of harming people and drawing their spirits away from God. They can see into the future and cause diseases, bad weather, or failed harvests. They can even slip into people's dreams.

And so there are bad females who, seduced by the whisperings of Satan, confess to riding at night with innumerable other women on certain animals. They fly about, looking for sexual partners. Or they kill small children (and even adults). They know the magic that makes people ill and robs men of their virility. They confuse the mind, poison the livestock or the crops in the field. They use magic potions and know poisons, they wear amulets that protect them and bring ruin to others. In any case, the witches are in league with the Devil.

The Devil. Just as Katharina knows that God is the embodiment of all truth and all good, she knows that the Devil and the demons are the embodiment of all evil. Anyone who hopes to fend off the Devil and his henchmen has to see through his tricks. And that is so hard to do, because the demons and the Devil are unholy angels who have fallen away from God. Since they have already lived for an eternity, they can draw on a wealth of experience that humans can never hope to match. They have many supernatural means at their disposal, with which they can do mischief to humankind. But no matter how incomprehensible their doings may be, even the demons are subject to the laws that God has laid down.

And therein lies the hope of humankind: Yes, with their tricks and illusions the demons can cloud people's senses, but they can never directly control human will. Where people live in the truth of faith, the demons have no trump cards left to play. Firm Christian faith, in association with human reason, breaks the demons' magic spells. They pale before the godly truth; their deceptions break up and dissipate like a fog.

Right now, by daylight and on the crowded Wittenberg market square, Katharina isn't afraid of demons anyway. Their power increases in the dark, in the sounds of the night, in days of fever and of gloomy thoughts. For then the senses are open to lying and deception, to sinful thoughts, to the Devil's whisperings.

Katharina knows all too well how often—in times of humiliation, of burning anger—the Devil and all his demons were sitting right on her shoulder. And that was just fine with her... And then her dreams: They follow Katharina right into her daily routine, and at times she is unable to separate day from dream. But all these fears and visions of the Devil have not diminished her steadfast love of God, of Jesus and Mary. For Katharina the world is God's temple, and the Devil manages only to sneak in once in a while and squat on the privy.

Katharina has had Ave make up a pan of ointment. Now she hurries across the market square with its noise, then turns onto the narrow alley that leads to the linen weaver's house. It is a gabled, half-timbered house like all the others on the alley. Katharina steps into the large open space that takes up the entire ground floor and serves as the living room. Linen is hanging from the ceiling by the stove rod to dry. There are boards along the walls, and on them plates, bowls, pots, and jugs. The family's clothes hang on wooden pegs. Hansjörg, the weaver, carries a bolt of linen outside and onto a large table, where he will cut a piece twenty cubits long for Katharina.

The weaver's eldest boy sits at the great loom. Skillfully he sends the shuttle whizzing back and forth. Katharina goes over to the massive bed in the corner of the room. It is a simple wooden frame with planks laid across it. Everything is in urgent need of a good washing, she thinks. But the weaver's wife is ill. She has boils on her legs, which Katharina coats with the ointment. The family's four smallest members snuggle in around their mother. Or they pick on the littlest one until she cries and the mother makes them stop.

Katharina is glad when she can get out of these dank

quarters. The weaver's wife is related to the Cranachs' cook. The cook says she used to be a lovely girl. Katharina has a hard time imagining it, when she thinks of the weaver's wife's sunken, weary face. There are a lot of sick people in the world; Katharina sees more sickness every day. Especially the dark alleyways are filled with moans and whimpers.

By now, Katharina has grown accustomed to the loud bustle of the market. It is the song of the world. The church bells sound as a reminder of the war against the Turks, the songs of the scholars and the children's choirs echo through the alleys. The animals the peasants bring to market bleat and grunt and stink. From the taverns come the drunkards' slurred voices and the sounds of brawling. Just keep moving—drunks make Katharina nervous. However, she loves the flying sparks and clanging of iron at the blacksmith's shop. The planing and hammering, the smells of glue and freshly cut wood that waft out of the carpenter's workshop. The clatter of the looms at the cloth maker's.

Katharina is beset by hawkers touting their wares. "Over here, lovely maiden, over here, people! Buy these magnificent painted horses, elegant dolls, gingerbreads, wafers, decks of cards. Cord for your undershirt, needles, brushes and combs, thimbles, purses. Here, people, buy my hot bacon cakes, I've got pancakes, too . . ."

"Right this way, anyone with an aching tooth! I break out all sick teeth, and it doesn't hurt a bit, right this way!"

A group of students approaches. They quarrel and get into a shoving match with the journeymen who are standing about in the doorways. "Gulden eaters, lazybones, strawheads."

When the students see Katharina, they doff their birettas. "Grace and peace to you, Catherine of Siena, grace and peace, Maiden Katharin . . ."

Katharina returns their greeting but keeps her eyes straight ahead. Why is everyone here in Wittenberg calling her by the name of a saint?

A woman who lived a hundred years ago, who fought passionately for her political goals within the church. Why give her, Katharina, that name? They call her that everywhere. Even Cranach does so on occasion, and Luther himself recently addressed her using that name.

But she asks no one. In the end, she can guess the reason. It is connected with the visit of the city councillors. Women shall remain silent in the congregation . . . But Katharina has no regrets. What she said, she said.

Upon returning to the house, she hears from Barbara that Luther has come to see Cranach. He brings the news that Ulrich von Hutten has died.

"Now they're both gone, first Sickingen and now Hutten too," says Barbara.

"Where did he die?"

"On the island of Ufenau, Luther says it's in Lake Zurich."

"Yes. He was thirty-five."

"He died because he kept company with bad women." Barbara is vehemently kneading the bread dough. Katharina fetches the tallow lamps from all the rooms. They need to be filled and furnished with new flaxen wicks. Cautiously she carries the lamps back to their shelves, places them gingerly into niches in the walls. Her thoughts are with Ulrich von Hutten. A curious melancholy overtakes her. She has heard much about the brilliant knight who (after also growing up in a cloister) received his poet's laurels from Emperor Maximilian at the age of nineteen. A knight, a fighter for God. And now all Barbara has to say about him is that he died miserably. But didn't he *live* magnificently? When Luther's books were being burned in Liège and Louvain, in Cologne and Mainz, Ulrich von Hutten wrote:

> Here burn the pious Luther's writings,
> For, God, they speak of your good tidings.
> For they your Truth articulate,
> Pure as you did this Truth create.
> Oh God, these good words on the pyre,
> Your teachings murdered with cruel fire . . .

Hutten stormed against the false papist teachings, against the truth being for sale and the German people being robbed. Against the violence being done Luther because he was preaching what is right.

And Hutten offered his help:

> I'll not spare my worldly goods,
> Nor balk if it should cost me blood . . .
> God always stands by one who's just,
> That much is sure, in Him I'll trust
> I've boldly dared.

He boldly dared—and lost. Katharina knows that Luther wrote an open letter to Hutten communicating his own anger: "I do not wish that the Gospel be fought for with violence and bloodshed. Through the Word the world is overcome, the Church sustained. But the Antichrist, too, as he began without arms, so will he be destroyed without arms by the Word."

Of course, that's true. Katharina has heard much about the horrors of war. Nothing (except the plague) terrifies her as much as fear of a war. She has heard how the soldiers murder and set fires, how they pillage houses and gardens. How they murder, without compassion, pregnant women, old men, children . . .

Ulrich von Hutten. The handsome picture of a man with a laurel wreath around his head is overcast by shadows of war's cruelty. Laurels and coat of mail—the laurel wreath is slight, but the mail is massive and heavy. As Katharina brings the tallow light to the living room, a man is just coming out the door.

She has never seen him before. He is tall, young, with fair hair that falls to his shoulders. His intelligent, dark eyes focus on Katharina in surprise. "You are Katharina of Siena, aren't you?"

Has anyone ever looked at her like that? It seems that suddenly she is standing in the light; she feels warm and good. Katharina doesn't know how long they stand looking at each other like that. (Later, she tries again and again to recall these first, precious seconds, so that she might retain them forever.) At first, she doesn't quite understand his name. Hieronymus Baumgärtner. For three years, from

1518 to 1521, he studied in Wittenberg. Then as now, in town to see to his friend Philipp Melanchthon, he slept under the latter's roof. This morning he has paid a visit to the Cranach family.

From now on, he comes by more and more often. When Katharina goes to market, she looks for him in every face. Now she too wears her long hair down; sometimes she holds it back off her forehead with a colorful band. She, who still helps to prepare meals in the kitchen, scarcely eats herself—so distracted is she. She has to watch out: just now she almost stirred that spoonful of honey into the vegetables instead of the dessert. Katharina's thoughts are with Hieronymus. Each morning as she awakes, she is instantly aware that he exists.

Hieronymus. Often, Katharina can't wait until he is again by her side. Spontaneous thoughts of him (and they occur amazingly often) send warm waves through her body. Often, too, they are brief, almost painful flashes. Then, when Hieronymus is there, Katharina grows calm; for a long time she feels nothing at all—or everything. They stand close together, each holding the other tight.

Katharina is only a bit shorter than Hieronymus, just enough so that she can snuggle her head up against the soft skin of his throat or (if she stretches a little) his cheek. Peace, aroma, warmth, a sense of being at home. And joy. Through his clothes she feels his powerful back; her hands wander and seek and find.

Katharina looks at Hieronymus. The most beautiful thing about him—his eyes. Bluish green or greenish blue, depending. Radiant, warm, deep—nobody else has such eyes. The lids a little heavy at the sides, making his face look pensive, and sometimes a bit sad. Now he looks toward the door, where apparently some sound is to be heard. Katharina sees his profile, the gentle nose—no one is as beautiful as he. When Hieronymus again takes her in with his radiant smile, she is all love.

When she is alone, she often asks herself where this unnameable joy comes from. From his hands, his soft mouth. (Hieronymus has perfect teeth; Katharina knows no other grown person who does not have decayed teeth. Happily, her own teeth are also healthy, but they are a bit uneven in the front, sad to say.) But everything about Hieronymus is beautiful. He says that he was a fat child and got teased a lot. The thought of this is instantly painful to Katharina. She tells Hieronymus that she would love him even if he were as fat as Elector Friedrich.

The very first time she saw Hieronymus, Katharina went running to Ave in the apothecary workroom. "Did you see him, Ave?"

"Katharina, you're all head over heels."

Ave is happy for Katharina. Sometimes they sit together as they used to, secretly, in Ave's or Katharina's room. As novices in the cloister, each shared in the sadness and loneliness of the other. With body and soul, they comforted each other. Once they were in love with each other, now each of them loves a man. So much that is unfamiliar, mysterious, sweet. One tells the other how beautiful she is. Especially Katharina wants to hear over and over that she looks sweet and young. Ave is just nineteen, but in January she, Katharina, will be turning twenty-five. Hieronymus is barely a year older. Often, especially on Sundays after church, Katharina looks anxiously at the younger burghers' daughters, sitting in the balcony with *Schapeln* of fresh flowers in their hair. They are fifteen, seventeen, or eighteen, and waiting for husbands.

Then Katharina sneaks a glance at Hieronymus. But her pounding heart can rest easy: Hieronymus seems to have eyes only for her. By now, everyone knows about them. Barbara and Lucas Cranach are happy for her. "I must hurry and paint the maiden before Baumgärtner fetches her off to Nuremberg," says Cranach.

Luther, too, knows that Baumgärtner is wooing Katharina. He is pleased, supportive, and probably also relieved. At any rate, he is always in a hurry. He is at work on his text *On Worldly Authority: To What Extent It Is Due Obedience.* He is also composing a new order of worship.

✦   ✦   ✦

Besides, Luther is deeply troubled that two adherents of the Reformation have been burned in Brussels. He has received news of it:

> On the day of July 1 everyone gathers at the market in Brussels. Stately magistrates from Louvain come as well. Brothers of the Minorite order carry the banner of the cross in solemn procession. Further participants include the professors of theology, as well as the abbots with their bishops' miters and croziers. All are seated on the great raised platform that has been erected in front of the city hall.

At the eleventh hour they are led across the market square. There are three of them. All from the convent of Augustinians in Amsterdam. The youngest has a lovely face and refined bearing. The two others look altogether too shaggy and bearded. Now they are led to the stakes that have been erected for them. The consecration as priest and monk is stripped from all three. They are now of the world. One of the three is led away.

The two who remain, Hendrik Voes and Johannes von den Eschen, are told to disrobe. They do this calmly. They testify repeatedly that they are dying as Christians. That they believe in the Holy Christian Church. They say that this is a day they have long awaited. Now they are naked but for their under-shirts. There is no need to tie them to the stakes; they embrace them freely. Now the fire is lit. It takes a very long time. By intention or by chance? As the smoke and eventually the flames rise, they sing the Te Deum Laudamus until finally the flames choke out their voices . . .

✦ ✦ ✦

Katharina sees Luther pale and deep in thought. She knows the ballad that he dedicated to the martyrs. Especially the final stanza she has committed to memory:

> Summer at the threshold stands
> And winter's now departed;
> Fields are filled with young green plants.

The one who all this started
He also will complete it.

Is Luther not afraid for his own life? In his sermon at the castle church, he concludes by saying: "I am aware that I have sung high and loud. Brought forth many things that men said could not be. Much have I attacked too sharply. But what should I do differently? I must tell the truth. I prefer to have the world and not God be angry with me. The most they can take from me is my life."

✦　✦　✦

Katharina speaks with Hieronymus, who is one of Luther's friends and an adherent of his doctrine. He reminds her that two years earlier, writing from the Wartburg, Luther called on all Christians to guard against uproar and rebellion. He was saying even then that the redressing of grievances must be accomplished through the word, and not through the uprising of *Herr Omnes,* the great mob.

"For uproar," says Luther,

> uproar has no good sense and commonly strikes more the innocent than the guilty. Those who truly understand my teachings make no uproar. They have not learned it from me. Summa summarum, I will preach it, I will say it, I will write it. But to compel, to press by force, that I will do to no one. I have been against indulgences and the papists, but without violence. God's Word alone have I advanced, preached, and written. I have done nothing else.

While I have slept, while I have drunk Wittenberg beer with my Philippo and Amsdorf, the word has done so much that the papacy has grown weak. No prince nor emperor yet has diminished it as much.

But Hieronymus also shows Katharina the verses that the Meistersinger of Nuremberg, Hans Sachs, has composed concerning the state of Christendom:

> Awake! the day is drawing near.
> In arbors green a song I hear;
> A most delightful nightingale—
> Its voice resounds through hill and dale.
> The night dips down toward Occident,
> The day ascends from Orient;
> The ardent red of dawning day
> Comes driving somber clouds away . . .

✦　✦　✦

Many love Luther, many hate him. So far, Katharina has known only bits and pieces of his work. But now, with the help of Hieronymus, she is learning more and more of the specifics, so that the connections are becoming clearer and clearer to her. Yet that seems unimportant now. All recedes before the incomprehensible event that she experiences anew every day—her love for Hieronymus. And his love for her.

With the Cranachs they go to the dance hall on the market square. Philipp Melanchthon and his wife, Katharina, Justus Jonas and his wife, whose name is also Katharina. Dr. Axt and Ave join them as well. Katharina and Ave are inside a dance hall for the first time.

The windows of the great, paneled room reach from just under the eaves to the ground. They are decorated with the coats of arms of Wittenberg's wealthiest citizens and with the coat of arms of the elector. Katharina can hear the fiddling and fluting as they cross the market square. She has taken Hieronymus's arm.

He is the handsomest and stateliest of all the men, thinks Katharina. Today he is wearing a doublet and loose breeches of a dark fabric with fine yellow silk in the slits. Katharina has learned that this attire is reserved for the nobility. Evidently, Hieronymus doesn't care. His curly blond hair shines; he wears no hat.

Katharina is proud. She knows: anyone who is invited to a public dance is part of society. Now the time is behind her when she was buried in the cloister. And she is no longer just a tolerated guest in the Cranach house. That time, too, is behind her. Now she is the fiancée of the wealthy patrician Hieronymus Baumgärtner of Nuremberg. She is out dancing with the most highly respected citizens of the city. Blissfully she presses close to Hieronymus. She no longer fears the richly adorned women and girls promenading about the hall to the sounds of the music, whirling to a roundelay. The women wear colorful silk dresses, some with low necklines. Some have tied up their hair with scarves and are wearing richly decorated birettas on top.

Katharina Melanchthon, daughter of a wealthy burgher family, walks erect in her skirt of black silk with light blue stripes. Her bodice, too, is light blue, as are the feathers in her hat. She nods briefly to Katharina; otherwise, she keeps to herself.

This is the first time that Katharina has seen her famous husband, Philipp Melanchthon, up close. In the streets of Wittenberg she has seen him often. He has always struck her as small, slender, and oddly sad. Today, however, he seems animated. His narrow, usually pale face, with high forehead and thin beard, is relaxed. His eyes, close together and strikingly large, return the sparkle of the sconces and candelabra. Melanchthon is twenty-six years old. (Katharina has learned this from Barbara Cranach.)

He is from the Palatinate, and did his studies in Heidelberg and Tübingen. In Wittenberg he lectures on Aristotelian philosophy, as well as the Greek and Roman classics. His uncle, Reuchlin, proposed him for the position here. Everyone knows that when Melanchthon lectures, the halls are filled. Luther calls him the best Greek, the most scholarly, most educated man. The two are close confidants and friends.

Luther has even said: "Maybe I am only the forerunner of Philippus, whose way I am to prepare in power and in spirit." And: "I was born that I might stand in the field and do battle with mobs and devils, thus are my books stormy and warlike. I am the great pioneer woodsman who must blaze trails. But Philipp moves about cleanly and quietly, sows and waters with pleasure, after God blessed him so abundantly with his gifts . . ."

This is what Katharina is thinking while she watches the famous humanist step onto the dance floor with Katharina

Jonas for a roundelay. Justus Jonas escorts Melanchthon's wife, and Katharina and Hieronymus take their places as well. Katharina follows the simple dance steps easily. Effortlessly. As she looks up at Hieronymus, she feels as though heaven and earth are dancing with them. It's as if, during those days and nights in the cloister that were so full of tears and loneliness, as if she had not given in completely to despair only because she had somehow sensed that God would send her this man.

"How great are your works, O Lord! Your thoughts are very deep." Katharina has said the Psalm aloud to herself.

"What did you say just now?" Hieronymus wants to know.

"Oh, nothing."

No one (not even he) must know that sometimes Katharina sits in her bed at night with tears of joy in her eyes. That she then prays: "Dear God, give me this man."

Melanchthon asks her to dance. As they move onto the dance floor, stepping in time to the music, he quotes: "I truly think they're fools and more / who find their fun on the dancing floor."

Katharina knows that one. Hieronymus gave her a book, *The Ship of Fools* by Sebastian Brant. "On Dancing," she read. "On Beggars." "On Becoming a Cleric." "On Blasphemy." "On Spiteful Women." "On Guarding Women." Katharina's eyes widened and her ears burned as she read:

> It's foolish days and aggravation
> If guarding a wife's your occupation . . .
> Mount a padlock on the gate
> Check each door and window grate

Hire guards on foot and horse
No matter! Things will run their course.

Albrecht Dürer made woodcuts to go with the verses. "On Guarding Wives" has a woman looking out a window, while men try in vain to catch a swarm of grasshoppers. Another man is pouring water into a well. The rhyme:

Go tend grasshoppers in the sun
To the well with water run
Who guards the woman he has won . . .

Yes, and she has read "On Dancing," too. She doesn't know the rhyme by heart, as Melanchthon does. But one couplet does occur to her:

A man takes Venus by the hands
And there all thought of honor ends . . .

A delighted Melanchthon continues from there:

Dance priest and monk with townfolk fine
Cowl and habit wait in line . . .

As they rejoin the others, still laughing, Melanchthon's wife turns directly to Katharina for the first time: "So dancing is pleasanter than praying, isn't it?" In her un-abashed joy, Katharina is about to answer that it's a thousand times nicer. Then she sees Ave's eyes. Confused, she falls silent.

Barbara Cranach suggests that they be going. She is

tired. Although the opulent and loose-fitting silk dress conceals her condition from outsiders, the pregnancy is causing her trouble.

Ave embraces Katharina emphatically as they say good night. Katharina Jonas (she is pregnant as well) also wraps her arms around her namesake: "You are lovely and gracious, Katharina von Bora; I wish you God's blessing." While she speaks, she is looking at Baumgärtner, and then she extends a hand to him.

Outside the Cranach house, Lucas takes Katharina's shoulders in his hands. He quotes an old expression: "If you want to stuff every unkind mouth, you'll need an awful lot of flour." The couple goes inside, but Katharina and Hieronymus stay in the courtyard awhile. They always find it hard to part company.

Katharina wants to know why Ave suddenly looked so sad. Hieronymus doesn't want to discuss it. "Oh, let's not make a river out of a little trickle."

Finally, though, he does tell her: "Melanchthon's wife was tight-lipped while you and Melanchthon were having such a good time dancing. Finally, she said: 'Evidently in the cloister they learn flirting better than liturgy.'"

Katharina can barely control herself. She would like to race the few steps to Melanchthon's house and take that spiteful woman by the hair and shake her. "May she go straight to Hell and lie forever between two millstones, ohhh . . ."

In her anger, Katharina almost forgets that Hieronymus is with her. He presses her close to him, gently strokes her face. "There are people who can't stand someone who is gracious. Because they themselves are not gracious. Like Katharina Melanchthon. She is basically a poor soul, unhappy in her constant envy of others. I feel sorry for Melanchthon. I love him like a brother. Why did he have to take that brittle old crab for a wife? I see how she blackmails him every day."

Hieronymus presses Katharina close once more. "Come, my heart. Don't give it another thought. After all, Jonas's wife just told you that you are lovely and gracious. Even my pale Philippus warms up to you. I'm almost jealous."

When he sees that Katharina's fists are still tightly clenched, he tenderly lifts her head. "You are a good person, Katharina, aren't you? And a truly good person would never ask a beggar why he isn't wearing a kingly robe, would she?"

These words occupy Katharina's thoughts for a long time. She doesn't know what a good person is. And she doesn't particularly care whether she is one. But the image of a beggar—that soothes her soul. Her imagination removes Katharina Melanchthon's silk gowns and dresses her instead in rags . . .

✦   ✦   ✦

Katharina and Hieronymus meet as often as they can manage in the meadows along the Elbe River. How good that it's still summer. Katharina takes care of the day's work—a constant to and fro, up and down stairs—as if she had wings. In the taproom she also balances the accounts, since the assistant can't read or write. She writes out a price list:

1 quarter measure Malvasia	5 Groschen
1 quarter measure Rhein Wine	18 Groschen
1 quarter measure Franconian Wine	14 Groschen

In the Cranach household, the help have learned to turn to Katharina when there's no more flour in the house or when fish for the noonday meal hasn't arrived at the market yet. Barbara's baby is overdue. She can scarcely get out of bed.

"I wonder why the baby won't come out." An anxious Katharina says this to Hieronymus.

"It doesn't want any part of our evil world," he says with a carefree laugh. He's in love. "Just wait until our children come."

Katharina's heart takes a mighty leap for joy. Is he going to talk about engagement now? Instead, Hieronymus begins to caress her. Gently but insistently his mouth presses her lips apart. His hands know their way around her dress. Each day her desire increases to feel his powerful hands on her skin. She is drawn to the warmth of his body, the aroma of his skin. She can't get close enough to it. She doesn't want to think about whether the pleasure she is feeling comes from God or from the Devil. And she doesn't know, either, why her thoughts keep wandering back to the cloister. She sees herself lying down in the chapter hall at her profession. Into the hands of the Reverend Mother she says her vows: "Mother, I promise you obedience in accordance with the rule of St. Benedict until death." To which the Reverend Mother replies: "And may God give you eternal life . . ."

Fear, remorse, pleasure—but the greatest of these is plea-sure. It is as if Katharina were drinking life itself from Hier-onymus's lips, her new life in the world. And she asks the good angels to stand by her and protect her against the demons. If this is of the Devil—what she is feeling in her body, what is permeating her body so that in the end it seems she exists only as pleasure, and as body no longer—if that is of the Devil, then the Devil is stronger than she.

Then again, Katharina thinks, nothing (at least, nothing on earth) can be more beautiful and more sacred than what she feels for Hieronymus. She looks at him, she can't stop touching him, feeling his cool skin beneath her hands. Like the finest silk. Once again Katharina presses herself against him. In the ecstasy of her desire she again sees the Rever-end Mother and the sisters gathered as a chorus. They call out: the vow, the vow . . .

Stunned, Katharina gets up, gently frees herself from his hands. The vow. She forgot to remind him about their engagement.

He brushes the tousled hair off his face, sits up as well, and looks squarely at Katharina. "You know, on Sunday after the service I'm journeying home. I will report to my father that we plan to marry. I don't want to take him by surprise with a formal engagement. You know, we should honor father and mother. Before Christmas I'll be back for us to be engaged. Then in May, I think, we'll have the wed-ding."

> Under the linden
> on the heath

he and I together lay.
There you'll be findin'
still there, both
grass and flowers in disarray.
Near the forest in the dale
sweetly sang the nightingale.

As Hieronymus walks Katharina home, dusk is already falling. They have to hurry; they have no lamp with them. The narrow alleys are already quite dark; through a window here and there they see pine shavings flaring up, or through the still-open upper half of a door the hearth fire glowing red.

Katharina is afraid in the dark; she runs faster. The night, with its eerie spirits and ghosts, bears in on her. On Sunday, Hieronymus is leaving for Nuremberg already. Sweet Mother of God, protect him.

Fear falls like a stone upon Katharina's heart when she sees two pitch pans set up in the courtyard on the Cranach property. What a commotion at this hour! Maids race to the well, the cook runs up to Katharina, her arms in the air. "Come, Miss, hurry."

"Barbara! Jesus have mercy!" Katharina flies up the stairs. Cranach and their two sons, Lucas and Johannes, are just emerging from the bedroom.

"It's not going well," Cranach mumbles.

The boys look pale, their eyes big and helpless. In the bedroom, the midwife presses on Barbara's belly. Ave bends down close to Barbara, holds her lovingly, wipes her forehead.

With a scream that pierces Katharina's ears, Barbara gives a sudden convulsion—and the child is there. It is dead. A girl.

✦   ✦   ✦

Ave and Katharina wash their friend, pull on a fresh linen gown. Barbara lets them do whatever they want. Once, she whispers, barely audibly: "It hadn't moved for a long time."

Outside the room, Katharina falls into Ave's arms, weeping. She blames herself. Why did she stay out so long? Why didn't she take better care of Barbara? Why didn't she sense that Barbara had been full of anxiety and worry for days? Oh, how love makes us selfish! Katharina feels like screaming out of shame and remorse. She is not worthy to live in this house. She's blind, insensitive to the fears of others, oh God!

The midwife comes with the bundle. Wordlessly she hands it to the two girls. Ave takes the dead child and carries it downstairs. Katharina slips quietly into Barbara's room. She sits down by her bed and takes her hand. She says a mute psalm:

> Do not be far from me,
>   for trouble is near
>   and there is no one to help.
> I am poured out like water,
>   and all my bones are out of joint;
> my heart is like wax;
>   it is melted within my breast;
> my mouth is dried up like a potsherd,

and my tongue sticks to my jaws;
you lay me in the dust of death . . .

But you, O Lord, do not be far away!
O my help, come quickly to my aid!

✦   ✦   ✦

In the days that follow, Katharina can't do enough to care
for Barbara and comfort her. Daily she spreads fresh linens
on her bed, shakes out the pillows, washes her bedridden
friend with rosewater. Every day Katharina ponders what
she might cook for her. Again and again she goes to the
market, buys doves, quail, or pheasants, which she fills with
aromatic herbs, in order to stimulate the patient's appetite.
She bakes bread from fine flour that she sifts several times.
She beats eggs, butter, and cream to make fluffy scrambled
eggs. With chopped almonds, honey, and cream she makes
candies.

Concern over the health of her hostess almost crowds
out the pain when Hieronymus leaves. In church this
morning, she spent a lot of time looking at him as he stood
beside Melanchthon in the men's section.

Luther was preaching. "David says in Psalm 51:5,
'Indeed, I was born guilty, a sinner when my mother conceived me.' That is the same as Augustine saying, 'Original
sin comes not from a person's origin or birth, it comes
from pleasure.' As if he wanted to say, if parents could con-
ceive and have children without pleasure and desire, then
no child would be born with original sin. But the Lord
God tolerates this pleasure and desire in the parents for the
sake of marriage, which he instituted, and for the multipli-

cation of humankind, but especially with an eye directed
toward baptism and belief in Jesus Christ, because pleasure
can never be taken away completely in this life . . ."

Katharina scarcely listened to the rest of the sermon.
Her eyes were on Hieronymus alone. To her, he represents
all pleasure and desire. But, most of all, love—to whatever
extent the three can be separated. How empty the church
will be without him. How empty the streets, the gardens,
the meadows along the Elbe.

Hieronymus has written out an old poem for her:

> You are mine
> I am yours
> Of that you can be sure;
> You are locked
> Within my heart
> The little key I've thrown away
> And ever after there you'll stay.

✦　✦　✦

Katharina has never seen Hieronymus on horseback. As he
rides into the courtyard, her heart hurts with joy. And with
sadness that he is leaving. He will need at between fourteen and eighteen days for the journey, depending on the
weather. Katharina can't allow herself to think about all
that might happen to him. It's true that anyone who
ambushes travelers is severely punished, yet the danger is
great. Thunderstorms could come up, Hieronymus could
take ill . . . Katharina feels miserable. She can't keep the
tears from running down her face.

Hieronymus kisses her, holds her tenderly: "By Christmas I'll be back, Katharina. And in spring, with the roses, we'll be married!"

Cranach, too, comes and bids Baumgärtner farewell. When he sees Katharina's tears, he takes her comfortingly by the shoulders.

"Come back soon," says Katharina.

"You have my word," Hieronymus replies.

Quickly he mounts his horse and rides out of the yard. Katharina feels like running after him. Like shouting, "Stay! Stay!"

Instead, she goes into the house.

Cranach stands in the yard looking out the gate. He is afraid that Baumgärtner won't come back. That he won't be able to come back.

3

WINTER COMES EARLY this year. Early winters mean hunger, cold, misery. The Elbe has a crust of ice. From beneath the ice come menacing gurgles and groans. Snowflakes dance. They cover everything that people need to live. Wood and tinder for the fire. Things that grow in the forest: blueberries, chestnuts, mushrooms, the bees' honey—everything has disappeared. There are no more beechnuts or acorns for the livestock. No building timber for shingles and boards, for shoes, tools, bowls, and spoons. No charcoal for smithing, no resin torches to light the rooms, no oak bark for tanning hides.

Winter is here. Ominous in snowy white, full of perils. Soon the cattle will be screaming with hunger in the stalls, and the children in the house as well. All reserves are used up. Especially since most of them had to be handed over.

Yet the word races across the land. The sermons. The pamphlets. The woodcuts. Evil scoundrels and crazy fools— that's what they're calling the authorities. "Evil scoundrels," that's what the gurgles and groans under the ice are saying. "Crazy fools," come the murmurs beneath the weight of the snow. We want some of the venison. Of the fish. Of the fowl. We want our wood. We want to be free like the Swiss, come the murmurings up and down the countryside. And the winter is cold, cold as death himself. He walks through the village in his fur-trimmed coat. Walks into the stalls, takes the livestock. He walks into the houses, the old, crumbling ones and the new, stately ones, no matter—he walks in and takes the peasant, the maid, the lovely girl, the child. He walks into the church and takes the sexton, saunters on through the gates of the city, and dances with the wealthy burghers to the tune of a fiddle.

Katharina, too, has seen him. But death brings her only a feverish dream: She sees golden angels with lutes and harps and zithers, all of them beautiful and looking at her with friendly eyes. And among the hosts Katharina sees many people, burghers, peasants, noblefolk, patricians, maidens and women. She searches for Hieronymus among them, but they all turn their back on her. They all look upward. When Katharina follows their gaze, she sees a great, golden throne covered with magnificent red-gold silk. And on the throne Mary, Mother of God. She is wearing a bright red gown, and over it a cloak of heavenly blue. Her long hair is in curls, her forehead high and white. How beautiful she is. At her side sits Jesus in a long, loose silk robe. It is white and immaculate. Like Mary, he is wearing a golden crown. And the angels play their music louder and louder.

Katharina wakes up. Her head feels as heavy as a millstone, her mouth is dry and has a bitter taste. She is aware of her every limb individually. What hurts most is her throat. She can hardly swallow. Only when she sits up in bed does she realize that behind her, on the only chair in the room, is Lucas, the Cranachs' younger son. He has evidently been sitting there a long time, plucking the strings of his hand harp and utterly lost in thought. Now he looks up at Katharina with a gentle, friendly smile. Lucas is blond. He has a delicate face with eyes that look at one in a curiously inquisitive way. His father has painted portraits of the boy, sometimes with black eyes and reddish blond hair, other times with blue eyes. His older brother, Johannes, has already begun his apprenticeship in their father's studio. Lucas still takes Latin lessons from Melanchthon, but he says that later he wants to be a woodcarver.

"You're ill, aren't you, Miss Katharina?" His inquisitive eyes are on Katharina.

Her head is pounding as she leans forward to begin combing her hair. Lucas sets down his harp and takes the comb from Katharina's hand. "Let me do that."

Katharina willingly lets him carefully part and comb out her long, dense hair. Through the veil of apathy she does feel the warmth of the careful, soft hand of this child. Tenderness. Love. The thought hurts. Katharina knows now how love begins. And how it ends, too.

✦   ✦   ✦

Christmas is long since past. And January, too, has just a few days remaining.

Hieronymus did not return. And the courier never brought word for Katharina. First there was the fear. Something has happened to him. Katharina writes a letter to

Nuremberg. Barbara, who happens by, says there's no point in sending this letter.

"Why not, Barbara, why?"

"Katharina, now I must tell you. Nuremberg is not Wittenberg. Baumgärtner's father is one of the wealthiest men in Nuremberg. He is a man of state. You know that marriage to a runaway nun is forbidden under religious as well as secular law. The penalty is death!"

"But Elisabeth Cruziger was a nun too. And Ave is going to marry, and Margarete and Veronika, I could name you so many . . ."

"Katharina, it's just not the same thing. Kaspar Cruziger is a Protestant clergyman, Dr. Axt lives in reformed Wittenberg—believe me, in Nuremberg the clocks run differently." Barbara goes to the window, looks out. Then she turns to Katharina: "Melanchthon told us that Baumgärtner's father has strictly prohibited the marriage. He has forbidden Hieronymus to make contact with you again. Otherwise he will disown his son."

Why doesn't the earth open up? Why doesn't it grow dark? Why doesn't a storm come and tear the roof off this house? Why, why, why?

Katharina pounds her fists against the wooden slats that line the walls of her room. She stares at the wood and knows that she'll get no answer. From anyone. She feels cold. So it's over. Her love, her hope, her pride, everything that she has built upon Hieronymus, it's all destroyed. Finished. Yes, she did carry her head high during her time with him. And in the time afterwards, too, she walked through the city like a queen. With a crown of joy.

And now? To the cross with her, nail the runaway cloister whore to a cross. Let her wear a crown of thorns and hang on the cross until all her haughtiness is gone . . .

The shame, the rage. Everywhere Katharina thinks she sees mocking faces. On the street, at the market, in church. Just look, look at the abandoned bride. Bride? They weren't even engaged. He was leading her on, what else? Who is she, anyway? Proud as a countess. She's nothing more than a runaway nun.

She runs a gauntlet of pointed lances, treading on sharp stones, and her feet are bare.

Why can't she cry? Grieve silently like Barbara did over her stillborn daughter?

All Katharina feels now is anger. And hatred that keeps growing and swelling within her. At night she tosses and turns in her bed, soaked in sweat. By day she goes about the house with lips compressed.

Her hate-filled imagination is constantly in Nuremberg. At the home of the elder Baumgärtner. She sees herself riding to Nuremberg disguised as a journeyman painter. Her hatred lends the horse wings. And so she finally reaches the famous city. People readily give her directions to the splendid Baumgärtner house. Katharina tears off her dusty biretta and her broad cloak. She asks for Hieronymus. But it's the father who confronts her. He laughs mockingly. "Hieronymus? He is out of the country. Do you really think I would leave him to the schemes and tricks of a cloister whore?"

Katharina sees his arrogant face. He has the same veiled eyes as Hieronymus. Yet in the father they seem oddly cold, as if he were blind. Baumgärtner is wearing an open cloth coat with a massive fur collar. He puts his hands on his hips, revealing an elegant tassel and a gold-studded belt.

Katharina would like to smash her fist into his smug face. Even in her imagination, she feels that she's drowning in hatred. In her thoughts she shouts at the old man: "You are filled with arrogance toward me. You dare call me a whore. All you know is haughtiness and money. Just who are you to push everything aside for the sake of your fame and your honor? My forefathers were settled on our estate at Lippendorf when yours were out in the streets hawking their wares. You think you're smart, but believe me, you're spinning the Devil's yarn. And so help me, as my name is Katharina von Bora, and as I am called Catherine of Siena, I will see to it that you and your house are all sent to Hell. For you, the Devil will stoke an especially nice fire, the demons will flay you and drag you on ropes across the coals, again and again. With red-hot tongs they will cure you of your arrogance once and for all."

Then she begs God to give her a gentle, humble heart. Yet the demons of hatred are stronger . . .

It takes a long while before Katharina's rages subside. The ring she wears on her index finger provides some help. A king's ring. He gave it to Katharina when he was in Wittenberg a year ago last fall and stayed as a guest in the Cranach home. Katharina recalls it often. Until then, she had never seen a king. Actually, he didn't strike her as regal at all. He rode into Wittenberg with a retinue of only two men. King Christian II of Denmark, who is married to Isabella, a sister of the Emperor. Once he wore three crowns on his head. Those of Sweden, Norway, and Denmark. But the Swedish nobility had opposed him. Christian got revenge for their revolt, but three years later he was driven out of his kingdom. He wanted his German relatives to help him. He came to Wittenberg because Elector Friedrich is also a relative by marriage. Above all, he came to profess his loyalty to Luther and to the Reformation. By doing so he hoped to find a way out of his predicament. That was in October 1523.

Katharina will never forget how they all walked together to the church service. The Cranachs, their sons, the servants, King Christian, and Katharina. He offered her his arm. His eyes were filled with sad tenderness. For every piece of bread she passed him, for every chalice of wine, he thanked her with his smile. When he departed, he embraced Katharina for a long moment and gave her the ring. They tried it on every finger until it fit her index finger. The ring is made of gold.

Hieronymus did ask Katharina about the ring. She answered truthfully. And he promised her a much more beautiful ring. She never got it.

Hieronymus. Katharina can practically see him laying everything onto the scales: here Katharina, there his father, the family, the fortune, the status. Now the scale on which Katharina is seated shoots upward. Weighed and found to be too light. So who is the real Katharina? The cloister whore or St. Catherine of Siena?

Luther, at least, is willing to help. He tells her that he wrote to Hieronymus, a while ago already: "By the way, if you want to keep your Katharina von Bora, then hurry, before she is given to another who is already at hand. She has not yet got over her love for you. I would surely rejoice to see the two of you united."

Luther got no reply from Hieronymus either.

Several times now, Katharina has been with Ave or Barbara to the Augustinian Hermit Cloister (locals call it the Black Cloister), where Luther lives. The first time Katharina was taken aback. This is supposed to be a cloister? It stands at the southeast corner of Wittenberg overlooking the Elbe pasture and consists actually of just one house for sleeping and eating, with a tower. There are a ground floor, two upper stories, and an attic. On the first floor, the windows are quite large; on the second, they're tiny. They face south onto the city moat and the Elbe pasture, and north onto the cloister yard. About forty monks lived here once. Now there remain only Luther, his prior Eberhard Brisger, and his famulus Wolfgang Sieberger.

At first, Katharina simply can't believe it. Compared with this Black Cloister, Marienthron is a princely castle! The abandoned cells here are musty and completely empty. Luther, Brisger, and Sieberger really do sleep on simple straw sacks. Barbara, Katharina, or Ave often bring meals to the Black Cloister, for their housekeeping, too, is extremely primitive. Luther tells Katharina that his beggar's sack has a big hole in it. He had to pay every monk who left the cloister a dower of one hundred gulden. The elector's inspectors have seized all the income. Luther's own salary has been cut as well.

While Katharina's mind is dwelling on the musty, joyless cloister, the thought occurs to her for the first time that

Luther, whose name is in the air all across Germany, the reformer who has the attention of Pope, emperor, kings, princes, and electors, lives in the most primitive of circumstances and is nothing more than a poor beggar monk. Not to mention his being excommunicated—an unparalleled injustice against a man who does nothing but work himself to the bone from dawn until night for God's truth.

Curiously, this thought leaves Katharina's heart feeling lighter. In her mind there is an idea, small as a newborn bird. But soon it begins to flutter its wings, preparing to take flight.

✦   ✦   ✦

Now Katharina gives young Lucas an affectionate pat as a thank-you for his kindness. It's as if he had done more than just comb her hair—as if his loving hands had removed the thicket of thorns from her heart as well. Katharina stretches her aching limbs and decides to draw a bath. There are still some dried rose petals left.

She asks Lucas to have the houseboy light the fire for a bath. The Cranachs have a large, bright bathing room, which can be warmed quickly by means of a massive fireplace. In kettles suspended over the fire, plenty of water can be heated and the supply replenished again and again. Dark blue tiles from Italy cover the floor of the bathing room. The large bathtubs are emptied into a drain beneath a wooden grate, and from there a pipe runs out of the house.

Barbara, attracted by the preparations, feels like having a bath, too. So do Cranach and little Lucas. Barbara washes Katharina's hair. Katharina has learned from her how to add rosewater, lavender, or chamomile to the soap they buy from the soap boiler. For Katharina's hair a lather of chestnut hulls is good, while Barbara's light hair is rinsed with a chamomile blend. Cranach and his son have the women wash and comb their hair, too.

Katharina loves the cozy warmth of the bathing room. Her cramped limbs relax; she begins to feel warm and content. While the women are still busy with their long hair, Cranach and his son sit down to a board game. Cranach junior wants his father to teach him to play chess. When their hair is combed out and the women have rubbed their skin with fragrant oil, they roll dice with the men and play cards until everyone's hair has completely dried in the warm air.

The game of chess reminds Katharina vividly of her Aunt Lene, actually Magdalene, mistress of the infirmary at Marienthron. She, like the abbess, is an aunt of Katharina's, though on her father's side. Aunt Magdalene always strictly avoided seeing Katharina as her niece. For one thing, doing so would have violated the cloister rules that forbade giving anyone preferential treatment. For another, she cultivated a reputation for dour energy, which may have come with her job, dealing with the sick. But, astonishingly enough, she was always ready to join in any scheme to break the rules. For example, Ave and Katharina loved to swim in the cloister pond. This was strictly prohibited. Aunt Magdalene herself avoided the water like the Devil, yet she made it possible for Ave and Katharina to slip out of the cloister on summer nights and go swimming. She would stand in the reeds like a big white hen and whisper an anxious "Psht! Psht!" when the girls' splashing and giggling got too loud.

The infirmary mistress would diagnose severe fevers, nosebleeds, and stomach cramps in perfectly healthy novices so that the girls could lie down in the infirmary and get their fill of sleep for once. And she found ways and means to sneak snacks to a girl sentenced to a strict fast.

She was an energetic participant in the nuns' plan to escape. Beneath her ample robe she smuggled pamphlets in and carried letters out of the cloister. Her surly demeanor toward all fellow sisters excluded her from any suspicion of conspiracy. Nevertheless, she herself did not want to leave the cloister: "Wherever would I go? I am a nun, and old besides. Both together is too much."

She was just as gruff in refusing any thanks. But she did stand watching at the garden gate until the fleeing girls had disappeared into the woods.

It is as if Katharina's thoughts had reached Aunt Magdalene. The courier brings a letter for her. Immediately she recognizes the seal of Cloister Marienthron. Aunt Lene writes that in this spring even more nuns have left Cloister Marienthron. No longer do they have to do so secretly. The Reverend Mother gives each nun the choice. And behold, my dear child, writes Aunt Magdalene, behold, now we read and discuss the writings of Dr. Martinus Luther every day. Our Reverend Mother thinks very highly of him.

Katharina will tell Luther of this. She asks Barbara for linen sheets for his bed. Barbara gives her one of Cranach's fine nightshirts as well.

"Take the maid along. She can help you clean up and heat the room for him. It will do him good." After a while Barbara adds softly, ". . . and do you good, too."

✦ ✦ ✦

Katharina finds Luther in his tower room. He is sitting at the table and writing. Everything around him—the benches, the console tables, the footstools—is full of paper and books. Two students and Prior Brisger are with him.

Luther is surprised that Katharina wants to make his bed and prepare him a bath. But he does not refuse; he even seems pleased.

The maid looks around the room and then the cells. She shakes her head: The great Dr. Luther lives in such squalor.

Katharina says nothing. This squalor is not so unwelcome to her. She senses within herself an unaccustomed ease, a quiet confidence. She is not in a hurry. She has time. She can wait and let things grow.

✦ ✦ ✦

In the next weeks and months it becomes a regular habit that Katharina attend to the most pressing needs at the Black Cloister.

Once she is late. Luther sends a pupil: Has the maiden Katharina been taken ill?

Barbara and Katharina exchange looks.

Katharina grabs her basket and hurries to the Black Cloister. She runs down the street, senses that the worst of the cold has broken. Spring is coming, and nothing will stay as it is. Everything will change, and this time it must change in Katharina's favor. She has been in Wittenberg almost two years now, knows her way around on the streets, but also on the back alleys. She knows many peasants. They are groaning under the backbreaking work, the yoke of serfdom. Often Katharina has seen and heard that the women and children suffer the most. The peasant, despairing and hopeless, spends his last pennies for beer. All that remains for those at home are curses and beatings.

Luther, who reprimands those who torment the peasants—the priests, the lords, the princes—Luther wrote the Gospels for them. He chased away the papists, he said that the last shall be first. The peasants want the old law, God's law. And no longer to pay the best tithe of the grain harvest, the living tithe of horses, foals, calves, lambs, pigs. No longer the little or dead tithe of hay, hops, strawberries and blueberries. And when the head of a household dies, no longer to give up the best head—the best cow or the best horse . . . They want to catch fish and crawfish in their ponds and go hunting for game . . .

Everywhere, in the alleys, at the market, in the eyes of the servants, who have many relatives in the countryside, everywhere one can sense that the peasants are on the move. *Dran, dran, dran.* Free pasture, water, forests, *dran, dran, dran.* The peasants are rising up in the name of God. They are following Thomas Müntzer, who has made clear to them in fiery speeches that they are God's chosen people. Luther, by contrast—according to Müntzer—merely flatters the princes. Müntzer, who got a post in Zwickau only when Luther recommended him, proclaims "personal revelation." And with his visions he turns to the poor, who listen to him. Since his sermons bring about unrest, he is chased out of Zwickau. He flees to Allstedt, a small town in Thuringia. There again he finds followers. He sends messengers out across the land with his teachings.

Katharina knows little about Thomas Müntzer. Only that Luther calls him an enthusiast. Katharina is much more concerned about the peasants. Back in the cloister she realized that they were being shamelessly exploited and oppressed. She had often got into arguments with Aunt Lene, who would say every time, "You have to squeeze the peasant, or he'll squeeze you." This thought always outraged Katharina. What she'd really like to do is march with the peasants.

But she fears war. As far back as she can remember, the nuns, the maids and laborers at the cloister, and now the servants of the Cranachs have been telling her horror stories about war.

She sees Luther seldom. He is traveling back and forth across Thuringia. He is afraid the peasant war could send the edifice of his Reformation crashing down before it is even finished. Daily he hears reports of the insults Thomas Müntzer is hurling at him. Müntzer calls him Brother Fattened-Pig, Brother Easy Life. Liar, stark fool, devious raven, godless scoundrel, Father Treadlightly, basilisk, archheathen, brazen monk, arch-rascal. And: "Sleep, dear flesh, I'd rather smell you roasted by God's wrath . . ."

Katharina is puzzled that Luther reacts to these attacks with complete confidence. And she knows that he hates Müntzer. Müntzer, in the meanwhile married to a former nun and father of a small son, grows more fanatic by the day. He has visions and calls upon "inward illumination" by way of the spirit. He has been preaching everywhere that he needs neither the Bible nor the sacraments.

Luther sees in Müntzer a dangerous mixture of mystic contemplation and political revolution. Muntzer wants reformation by the sword. He teaches the peasants the mercenaries' battle cry: "*Dran! Dran! Dran!*"

✦   ✦   ✦

Katharina helps Luther prepare for another journey. She has baked him a couple of flatcakes and brings him a leather wine bottle. She hears him dictate a letter to the dukes: "This Müntzer, Satan that he is, has made himself a nest in Allstedt."

Luther wants to travel throughout Thuringia and preach against the enthusiasts. He sees that his gospel is in danger. Especially now, when the word is coursing throughout Germany and being victorious without a single blow of the sword.

Every time Luther returns from his sermons, he is despondent, furious. The people in the churches received him silently and mistrustfully. Others cursed him, laid a mutilated crucifix before him in the chancel.

The peasants are disappointed with Luther. They can't understand his admonitions to seek peace. And, worse still, he recommends that they submit even to unjust authority. Luther threatens, "He who takes up the sword shall die by the sword."

The princes and lords harbor ill will toward Luther as well. He has reproached them for misusing their offices and for violating their obligation to care for and protect their subjects. "God's wrath will be upon you . . ."

For the first time, Luther is helpless. Prayer and debate are no use against the crying injustice the peasants face. But he has no other weapons.

Luther's friends rarely come to the Black Cloister any more. Katharina often sees Luther worrying at his desk or wandering aimlessly about the cloister cemetery. She sees it, and feels an undefined affection, a sense of compassion for this outcast who carries on his struggle in absolute solitude.

✦   ✦   ✦

In the night, Brisger pounds at the Cranachs' gate. "Martinus is ill, come quickly."

Cranach pulls on his boots, Katharina wraps herself in a shawl. They race to the Black Cloister. Luther is in his bedchamber, a candle casts shadows. Wet with sweat and groaning, the sick man tosses and turns on his mattress, screams suddenly, claws with his fingernails at the white plaster of the wall.

His kidneys. Katharina makes him a large pot of tea and asks Brisger to bring a lot of water from the well. Again and again she urges Luther to drink a lot of tea. Beside himself with pain, he obeys. When the attack lets up a little, Katharina asks him to hop up the stairs to the very top and then back down again. (She learned of this treatment at Cloister Marienthron, where the sacristan suffered from kidney stones.) Luther does what Katharina suggests. In the meanwhile, she spreads fresh sheets over his bed. Cranach prepares a tub for him.

Sure enough, Luther is feeling better soon; especially the bath refreshes him.

Cranach goes back home. Katharina stays with Luther.

The patient is now lying peacefully in his bed. Only occasionally does he moan softly. Katharina sees his exhausted face, gently wipes the fine beads of sweat from his forehead and his upper lip. Luther looks like a child. Sad, vulnerable, alone.

Katharina, who has known for a long time now that she intends to win Luther over for herself, who is prepared to resort to any trickery, stands ashamed in the face of his defenselessness. Deep within herself she finds the desire to build a bridge to this solitary, pain-ridden man who reveals his pure, childlike soul as he sleeps. Katharina knows that she will swim to the shore of his soul, no matter how far from it she is today.

Softly she strokes his hands.

Suddenly she is aware that Luther is awake. That he is looking at her. She returns his gaze. Two solitary people. When Katharina has to look away, she lowers her head until her mouth softly touches his cheek. She stays bent over him until he wraps his arms firmly around her.

Katharina lies still. She hears his heart. Its steady beat has a calmness about it that reminds her of the stars. The stars of the night sky and their ever-constant courses. In their unalterable order they trace their paths across the firmament. They are one with the infinite vastness that holds and protects them. They are one with the unchanging laws of all life.

4

─────

IT IS MAY 5, 1525. Katharina is sewing new trousers for the Cranach sons. Barbara sits at the distaff. Cranach bursts into the room: "Elector Friedrich has died. Our kind lord is dead."

Katharina, too, is deeply shocked. Martinus! What a blow this must be for him! He owes the elector his life. Elector Friedrich of Saxony saw to it that Luther faced a diet in Germany, and not in Rome (which at that time would have meant either confinement to a cloister or burning at the stake if he didn't recant). The elector brought the outcast monk to safety at the Wartburg.

Katharina saw Elector Friedrich several times at church in Torgau and Wittenberg. What a splendid man he was. The curls of his formidable beard nearly hid his full, soft mouth. Intelligent, dark eyes looked distant, contemplative. With his elaborate biretta and his doublet trimmed with fur, the elector radiated an aura of power, steadiness, goodness, understanding. Katharina's heart has belonged to him ever since she read the open letter he wrote to his brother in April concerning the peasant uprising: "Perhaps we have given the poor folk cause for such revolt... Since the poor are burdened in many ways by us, the secular and religious authorities."

Holy Mother of God, who will protect Luther? Will all their plans now come to nothing?

Filled with secret anxiety, Katharina goes to the Black Cloister. Justus Jonas is there, Melanchthon, Bugenhagen, and Veit Dietrich.

Katharina sets to work in the primitive kitchen until the men leave. Then she rushes in to Luther, who takes her into his arms. Katharina clings to him fearfully. Yet Luther comforts her. No, he does not fear for his life. Katharina shouldn't be afraid, either. Not for him and not for the future. They'll be married, to spite the very Devil.

Katharina is immeasurably relieved. Now she has no more doubt of Luther's promise to take her as his wife. She secured this promise from him one day. The idea of asking Luther for his hand if need be came to Katharina in the winter—on her twenty-sixth birthday to be exact. She had worked herself into a genuine panic. How old was she supposed to get—without a husband, without a family, without a future?

She discarded the idea as preposterous, again and again. No, Luther will have to take the first step himself. She will steer him in that direction, she is doing all she can to that end already, but to suggest marriage—impossible!

Then one day she does it after all. Before going home, she tells Luther that his evening meal is ready on the stove. And suddenly she hears herself add: "I think you ought to marry me."

Her heart pounds; she feels the blood rushing to her head. At the same time her defiance is aroused. What has she got to lose? And he—he can only gain by it as well. If only he would open his mouth!

But Luther does not speak. He goes on writing, then looks up with eyes alert. Then he gives a lame little smile and asks whether Maiden Katharina of Siena would permit him to sleep on the matter.

Katharina leaves without a word. As she is about to step from the cloister yard onto the street, she hears footsteps behind her.

"Katharina!" It is Luther, and he takes her by the arm and draws her gently to him. He tells her that he accepts her suggestion. And does so with great pleasure. All the while, lights are dancing in his eyes.

Luther went and got his parents' approval in April. Just for that purpose he traveled to Mansfeld, and his parents sent their regards to Katharina. They will come to the wedding. Thank heavens! It is quite clear to Katharina that the elder Luthers are just about the only people who are glad to see him marry Katharina von Bora. The runaway monk and the runaway nun! Even Luther's closest friends are horrified. They would like to see Luther married, but to someone else—not to Katharina von Bora!

But Katharina has come to know her Martinus. Obstacles just focus him more intently on his goals. She knows that if rebellious peasants or raging princes don't kill him, he will keep the promise he made to her.

Katharina would rather have heard different wedding music than the crashing of lances and halberds, the screams of the wounded. In March and April the peasant hordes were still triumphing. They conquered large areas and laid them to waste. Hundreds of cloisters burned, monks and nuns murdered and defiled. The hordes breached fortresses and plundered them. Counts too, and knights, came along for the booty. (Later they would say they had been forced to do so.)

Massacres, burning, ravaging—those are the harbingers of spring in 1525. From Augsburg come the twelve main articles, with which the peasants make a desperate attempt to defend their demands, now being slandered by members of the old faith as wicked fruits of the new gospel. No, the peasants pointedly stress: the cause of the troubles is not the gospel but the Devil, suppressing the Word of God, which teaches love, peace, and unity. And: "Did the Lord hear the children of Israel who cried to him, and deliver them out of the hands of Pharaoh? Can he not save his own people today as well? Yes, he will save them. And soon!"

The peasants are filled with courage and hope and hatred. Not a few counts and lords take off their feathered hats to the peasants, salute the peasant flag, make all sorts of promises (and then, later, they will oppress the defeated peasants all the more cruelly). And: "As just as the cause of the peasants is, the means they use are often enough of the Devil."

The post courier brings word from Württemberg how the peasants played havoc among the aristocrats. He reports:

> The count of Weinsberg takes many of the noble-
> men and goes into the town. After he leaves, the
> peasants storm his castle so quickly that the noble-
> men aren't able to return in time. So the peasants
> capture the countess and her children and plunder

the castle. Then they move on to the town. The people of Weinsberg, in good peasant fashion, open the gates to them.

Then it's as if Lucifer and all his angels had been set loose. The peasants rampage like ones possessed. Count Dietrich von Attenberg flees into the church and up its tower. When he begins to speak from there and promises the peasants a lot of money, someone shoots at him. And others race up the tower and throw the count over the ledge. After that, they take thirteen noblemen, among them Helfenstein, Sturmfeder, Eltershofen, and Ruchzingen, to a field by the road to Heilbronn. There they form a circle and chase their lordships and their squires through the gauntlet, twenty-four men. The count of Weinsberg offers them a barrel of gold if they let him live. Nothing helps. When the count sees this, he stands perfectly still until they stab him to death. Eltershofen enters the ring with arms outstretched and goes willingly to his death. In violation of every rule of warfare, the peasants chase the noblemen through the gauntlet, then take their clothes and leave them naked where they lie. Almighty God have mercy upon us. After that, the peasants set fire to the castle and move on to Würzburg.

No, it's not a lovely wedding hymn the peasants sing for Luther and Katharina von Bora. Katharina knows that Luther is always expecting to be killed by the insurgents. She admires his fearlessness and calm. Still, it makes her furious that he isn't more careful, does not conceal himself. What will become of her if they kill Luther? One thing she does know: If they make Luther run the gauntlet, as Thomas Müntzer wishes, then she will go with him.

The lancers' war cry for hand-to-hand combat, *"Dran! Dran! Dran!"* comes closer and closer. Thomas Müntzer and Heinrich Pfeiffer, a former monk who used to preach in the town of Mühlhausen and has many followers, these two leaders of the peasants have gathered an army. Müntzer shouts, and the echoes resound throughout Thuringia, *"Dran, dran,* while the fire is hot. Don't let your sword grow cold. Hammer ping ping ping on Nimrod's anvils. *Dran, dran,* as long as you have daylight!"

Luther is beside himself with anger. Again he travels through Thuringia and the Harz, preaching in the churches. The people's rejection of him is, if anything, stronger than before. Once they even try to pull him down from the pulpit.

Deeply distraught and full of helpless rage, Luther finally returns to Wittenberg.

A clerk who accompanied him reports to Katharina, still outraged and trembling with fear as he recalls: "We were right in the middle of them. You should have seen their faces. Huge noses, glinting eyes, mouths foaming with hate. They carry around bells. Every time Dr. Martinus began to preach, they rang their bells. Had just one of them drawn his sword, there would have been a bloodbath."

Now the swords and lances are clashing throughout the land. The days have put aside their rough winter coat.

Everywhere delicate, new green is emerging from the ground and from the branches of the trees. But everything is drenched in blood. In Württemberg, in the Alsace, in Franconia, everywhere, the once-victorious peasants are being defeated. The executioners are setting about their work. The cruelty of the mercenaries who now come flooding back from the Pavia campaign far exceeds that of the peasant armies. Thomas Müntzer's *"dran, dran"* is silenced forever at the battle of Frankenhausen. Five thousand peasants dead and only five men lost on the princes' side. Many residents of Frankenhausen are mistreated and killed. Thomas Müntzer hides in a peasant house. He is discovered and captured. So is Pfeiffer. The thumb screws and Spanish boots await the two of them. After brutal torture they are beheaded, and their heads mounted on stakes outside the town.

So much death, so much blood.

Trembling with rage, Lucas Cranach reports how the princes took revenge against the Franconian sculptor Tilman Riemenschneider for supporting the peasants: they crushed the man's hands.

In Nuremberg, Albrecht Dürer designs a memorial column for the defeated peasants. He also draws a weeping peasant woman, abandoned and without possessions, seated at her distaff.

Katharina can't take in all these images. Her head is empty. Too empty to think, too empty to pray. She just wants the thirteenth of June to arrive, the day she is to have her wedding.

On top of everything else, she misses Ave. Ave has moved away with her husband to the court of Duke Albrecht of

Prussia, whom he now serves as personal doctor.

Katharina writes to Ave.

Grace and Peace in Christ. Dear Ave,

Thank you for your letter, and especially for the splendid headband with the flower of pearls. Never have I seen such a beautiful piece of jewelry. They wear such things at court, don't they? And now you're giving it to me! Oh, Ave, do I deserve it? Well, as far as you personally are concerned, my heart is pure. I love you sincerely, and you know it. But what about the rest? Who am I, Ave? Some say I'm a conniving nun who has gone out and snared Luther. Simon Lemnius—the one that Martinus relegated from the university for slandering Melanchthon—he writes that now that Luther has used me, he just wants to be rid of me. That actually he is attracted to you, Ave, or to some maiden from Magdeburg. No less than Erasmus of Rotterdam trumpets in all directions that I am expecting a child in a few weeks, and that's why we had to hurry up and get married now . . .

But, Ave, who am I really? Am I what the others say of me, or am I what I know of myself (and what you know of me)? Am I the proud, haughty, treacherous nun?

Or am I the passionate, restless, captive Katharina who needs love and trembles daily with rage at each new insult?

Who am I, Ave? Could I be the one today and the other tomorrow? Am I both at once?

Ave, the thirteenth, my wedding day, will be a great

day in my life. Probably the greatest of all. God bless you. Pray for your Katharina.

In Wittenberg, on the eighth of June in the year 1525.

✦　✦　✦

June 13, 1525

A Tuesday. Tuesdays are good for weddings. So they say. Katharina is awake very early. She has slept fitfully, and had confused dreams: Dressed in her bridal gown, she goes to the church. All the bells are ringing. From the alleys come other brides. Katharina sees that it's Ave, and Ave Grosse, too, and Margarete and Magdalene, Else, and Laneta, all going to the church with their husbands-to-be by their sides. Suddenly Katharina realizes that she is alone, that she is going to the church without Luther. They won't marry me without him, she tells herself, and so she turns back. In her room she takes off the bridal gown and thinks maybe she can give it to the maid . . . Holy Virgin, what can that dream mean? Surely Luther wouldn't . . .

No. Katharina shakes out her hair (in the two years since her escape it has grown long and plentiful), then combs it carefully and scrubs her teeth with chalk powder. Just as she did that day ten years ago. Back then, she was being married to God:

Katharina is fifteen years old. She and the other candidates are dressed in wedding gowns by the sacristan. Each wears a long, white dress and a veil with a bridal wreath. When they are all dressed, they are permitted to see their families one more time, to say good-bye. No one from

Katharina's family is there. She must make the big decision without the blessing of her parents. As if Katharina had a choice. She is not the only one among the candidates who thinks back on her parental household mainly with anger: God give a ruined year to the man who is making a nun of me.

Now the bells toll; the brides of Christ step from the cloister proper into the church. Katharina feels like a blind woman groping in the dark. But one thing she does grasp: today she must give herself away—to a community in which she has lived for a long time, but to which she nevertheless does not belong. In her mind, she must be one with the community and she must desire this to be so. She must renounce thinking her own thoughts, going her own ways. She must follow the intentions and ways of the abbess. She must join in the prayers rather than talking, she must obey rather than making decisions for herself. Deep within, Katharina rejects all this passionately. She lacks the necessary humility, and they keep telling her this, too: you lack the gift of humility . . .

Katharina receives Holy Communion. "Forgive me, O Lord, forgive me, sweet Mother of God." She throws herself down—like all the others—onto the steps of the altar and answers the priest's questions: "What do you desire?" "God's mercy and that of the order." Then the priest hands them the burning candle and the crucifix and gives them their new names. Katharina is now called Benedikta, as a sign that the world is closing its gates and she is entering a new life.

Now they all return to the cloister proper. In the chancel the disrobing ceremony is carried out. Katharina-Benedikta's long hair falls under the scissors of the novice mistress. She exchanges the secular bridal gown for the consecrated garment of the order, the white habit of St. Bernard.

✦   ✦   ✦

That was ten years ago. For a moment it seems to Katharina that a fragrance is passing through her room, the scent of the cloister, which she sometimes thinks she's smelling again in church. A faint, delicate scent of incense, wine, and clean linen—the unmistakable aroma of Catholicism.

Katharina opens the window. It is the time of the hay harvest. In the morning light she sees the broad pasture and the peasants with their scythes. She smells the aroma of the fresh grass, sees the mounds of hay raked together by the women and already beginning to dry. The women wear white scarves tied around their heads, as the sun is already quite high.

After the noonday meal, Barbara takes Katharina to a room. There are stacks of linen, hand towels, blankets, pots, dishes, drinking vessels—a generous dowry in the best of taste.

Katharina is speechless. Barbara gently touches her cheek.

Katharina dresses. Over the carefully bleached underdress she wears—today for the first time—a close-fitting corset and a wide skirt of the finest rose-colored fabric with interior facings of blue silk. It falls open in the front and lets the white underdress be seen. Barbara puts

Katharina's hair up and drapes a piece of spiderweb-fine silk over the headband, Ave's wedding present.

Katharina steps up to the mirror. She sees a high, smooth forehead, the eyebrows making a broad curve above the straight, narrow, rather long nose. The mouth is rather small but finely drawn. It is firmly closed, a cautious mouth, but the corners point upward.

"If I were a poet, I would sing of you that you are beautiful like an angel, like a garden full of flowers in bloom." Cranach has come up behind Katharina and is looking at her in the mirror. Beside his admiring eyes, Katharina feels for an instant that she is beautiful. That would be on account of the veil.

Cranach takes her by the shoulders. For several seconds he looks at her despairingly. "I cannot paint your beauty, I simply can't. Because your character is stronger than your beauty, that's why I can't paint you."

Lucas and Barbara Cranach walk with Katharina the few steps to the Black Cloister, where the wedding is to take place toward evening. The couple take Katharina between them, and the servants, loaded down with the dowry, follow. The people of Wittenberg watch the procession wide-eyed. The castle provost, Justus Jonas, arrives at the Black Cloister at the same time as the bride. He embraces Katharina briefly and passes on greetings and congratulations from his wife. Johannes Bugenhagen races up, and with him the jurist Johann Apel. These three. Luther has not invited Melanchthon. Katharina asked him not to, since Melanchthon is one of those who pass harsh judgment on this marriage.

"Be strong in the Lord and in the strength of his power," Bugenhagen preaches from Ephesians 6. "Above all, take the shield of faith, with which you will be able to quench all the flaming arrows of the evil one. Take the helmet of salvation, and the sword of the Spirit, which is the Word of God."

As the highest-ranking clergyman in Wittenberg and Luther's closest adviser, Bugenhagen conducts the wedding itself as well. He lays the hands of the bride and groom together. Luther's wedding ring (a gift from the elector, as is Katharina's) is a golden double band, and inlaid into the top of the raised twin bezels are a diamond, symbol of steadfast fidelity, and a ruby, symbol of pure love. The double band as well as the bezels can be pushed apart. Then the letters MLD, Martin Luther, Doctor, can be seen. Under the ruby, on the face of the shank, are engraved the letters CVB (Catharina von Bora). Inside, the two bands read: What.God.joins.together.let.no.man.part. Mounted on Katharina's ring is a ruby. Inside the band, it reads: D. Martinus Lutherus, Catharina v. Bora, 13 June 1525.

Katharina puts the ring onto Luther's finger. He wears it next to his golden doctoral ring. As Luther slips the ring onto her finger, for a moment Katharina feels exhausted, like after a long run. She has given a content to her life. Whether or not it has meaning, or ever will have, is something she has not thought about yet, and she doesn't want to in the future, either. She has no choice; she has never yet been able to choose. Not when she was the bride of Christ, and not today, either. And she knows that things don't stand much differently for Luther. He didn't choose

Katharina freely, either—who would know that better than she? But now they are wedded in the name of God and of Jesus Christ and in the presence of Wittenberg's highest clergy. Period. She is Katharina Luther. Now she just has to see it through to the end.

✦   ✦   ✦

According to the old custom, the newlyweds must now go to the nuptial bed in order to consummate the marriage in the presence of witnesses. In the bedchamber three candles are burning. They yield a soft, veiling light. Katharina noticed at the exchange of rings that Luther was restless; his hands were trembling. Now, as she lies close to him, she hears his heart beating again. This time, though, it is pounding hard, like after a great exertion—or out of fear.

Luther is all monk. Katharina was never all nun. Nor does she ask whether the presence of the witnesses will hinder her. She knows only that she must help her husband, and she will. That it is justified, and with good reason. Then, when the quiet pain does come, she takes a deep breath. And she has an inkling that completely uncharted territories, unknown riches, lie in that which until now she has more feared than looked forward to . . .

✦   ✦   ✦

Katharina wakes up very early. Whenever she eats just a little, and yesterday she scarcely felt like eating, she wakes up early the next day. Beside her, Luther is still sound asleep. He has rolled onto his side and pulled up the covers so tight that only his disheveled hair can be seen.

Quietly Katharina gets up and goes into the kitchen, which is more like a soot chamber. Evidently the ruins of what it must have been, when no fewer than forty monks lived in the cloister. Anyway, now it is empty and dirty. Besides the one fire site at the hearth there is nothing left. At least the maid has swept it out. Katharina sighs when she fails to get a fire started. She thinks of Barthel, who tends the ovens at the Cranach house. How skillful he is. Not to mention the stoker at Marienthron. Katharina can almost see him hurrying down the corridors at the cloister, always carrying massive loads of firewood.

Now—the tinder has caught fire. While the little flames grow larger and more and more lively, Katharina looks in her bags for her tooth powder. She gives her teeth a good rubbing and then combs her hair thoroughly. While she is combing, she tilts her head forward. In this position, Katharina believes, she does her best thinking. First of all, this pounded clay floor where she is standing will get stone or ceramic tiles. Anything else would be just patchwork. Even that little bit of washing and tooth rinsing has made a dirty puddle. So then, the kitchen needs to be tiled, the walls whitewashed. A chimney needs to be built for the smoke, an oven for making bread. And a bathing room is an absolute necessity. Wherever did the Augustinians bathe? Katharina found a solitary bathtub in one of the cells. Again she thinks with a sigh of the Cranach house and of Marienthron. Relieving oneself in the Black Cloister requires quite a bit of courage. A loose beam over a pit. She would much rather disappear outdoors. But Brisger and Sieberger are still in the house, and who knows what other suspicious eyes are watching the Black Cloister.

So, that's what Katharina will take care of first. Beneath the pestilentially stinking cesspool a water line must be laid that will rinse away the wastes. Anything else would be unbearable. She wants pipes of lead and wood—like the ones she knew at Marienthron—that will direct water for cooking and washing into the kitchen. She wants a pantry for supplies, she wants, she wants, she wants . . .

For a moment it seems to Katharina as if she has to climb the face of a huge cliff rising directly in front of her, and do it barefoot. She feels small and helpless and timid. But just for a moment. Then her ever-ready anger is at hand to plant her hands on her hips.

I am now Katharina Lutherin. No longer the idle bride of Christ, no longer the compliant houseguest of the Cranachs. And you watch, Wittenberg, here I come. I'll show you what it means to have a Dr. Martin Luther within your walls. The great, world-famous reformer who fills your university to the point of bursting, makes your professors, your printers, and your painters rich and your city coffers full. You city councillors who are so proud to have my Martinus here, you have let him live here in the dirt. But now that's enough of that. I'll teach you—you're not getting your Dr. Luther for free anymore.

Her plans give Katharina wings. She sets to work and makes a racket, and doesn't even notice that a man, looking sleepy and apparently perplexed, has shuffled into the kitchen. Wolfgang Sieberger, Luther's famulus. Until now, he has always hid when Katharina came to the cloister with the maid. He is afraid of women, afraid of work; he is afraid of everything that moves quickly. But he, too, needs something to eat in the morning, and anyway, Frau Doktorin is here to stay now. And so he steps aside with a sort of bow when Katharina turns to set things from her dowry onto the dusty shelves.

"So, Wolf—want to help me get the morning meal started?"

Actually, he doesn't want to, but what's the use? Sieberger, who actually is in charge of the inkhorns, the quill pens, the knives for erasing, and who finds even this much a burden and an imposition, suddenly finds himself sifting flour. Twice he should do this. After that, he tries to sneak out of the noise-filled kitchen. But Katharina amicably shows him how to mix the flour with salt and milk to form a dough. Holy St. Augustine, what a day!

Katharina explains to him that Luther has invited the wedding guests to come for a morning meal. "If you don't help me, Wolf, then the gentlemen will sit down to an empty table!"

So what? That wouldn't bother Sieberger. He'd much rather help himself to a crust of bread and a cup of milk and be left in peace.

But in her thoughts Katharina is already exchanging his filthy rags for new clothes. She will see to it that he gets a regular pair of leggings and a jerkin.

With a sigh, Katharina remarks that it is one thing to provide for a bachelor with things from the well-appointed Cranach house, and quite another to prepare a morning meal for dignified guests in an utterly desolate kitchen. Everywhere things are lacking. There aren't even eggs or milk. Would Wolf go to the market for her?

As if he hasn't done enough. Then again, a stroll down to the market does sound better to him than all this hustle and bustle.

"Where's the housekeeping money, Wolf?"

He brings her a small, black, iron chest. It is empty.

Katharina looks at Wolf, dumbfounded. He scratches his head, shrugs his shoulders. No money—that's the normal state of things at the Black Cloister.

Katharina goes to Luther. It's time that he got up. He's not in bed anymore.

Finally, Katharina finds him in his tower room. Didn't he hear her coming? Anyway, he is searching and shuffling through sermons and tracts. When she touches his shoulder, he manages only an "Oh, is that you?"

Katharina senses his embarrassment, of which she is not entirely free herself. Yet she has no time to deal with it; in an hour at most the guests will be here. "I need money," she says more brusquely than might befit a bride the morning after the wedding.

"Money? Oh yes, well, ahem, where do we have . . . ?"

Again the hunting begins. Books are lifted, texts, scrolls. Katharina joins in the search. And sure enough, in this mess they find two groschen, eight pfennige that she can press into the flour-covered hands of the famulus.

Katharina has discussed with Barbara well ahead of time what there should be for this morning meal. Most of the provisions came from the Cranach house. In a mortar, Katharina crushes almonds for the almond milk she so loves. Dried wheat kernels are boiled and served with butter and cinnamon. Hotcakes with sweetened cream and preserves of last year's cherries in honey. In the pan there are eight doves browning in butter. Katharina coughs on account of the smoke; she feels like her head is going to burst from constantly working over the hearth fire. And Wolf doesn't come back from the market.

Finally, Katharina puts her head into the bathtub. That feels good. Then there's a banging at the door. Two boys carry in several pitchers of wine. "From the city council," they say—and go banging off again.

"That's more like it," thinks Katharina, and she wipes the water from her face.

When the guests arrive, near the eleventh hour, everything is set. Jonas, Bugenhagen, Apel, and Lucas Cranach sit down at the table, while Barbara helps Katharina serve the dishes. Luther says that the official church wedding, to which his parents, Spalatin, Koppe, Amsdorf, and Link will come, will be on the twenty-seventh of the month, another Tuesday. "I am hoping that the angels will laugh then and the devils cry," he remarks sarcastically. And: "Now all the lords, the priests, and the peasants are against me. So be it: if they are furious and foolish now, I'll make them even more furious and more foolish."

Defiance, rebellion, protest—that is Luther's mood. "With my marriage to Katharina von Bora," he says, "I have stuffed the mouths of the slanderers."

Wrong. They go on screaming for years. Even the murderous Henry VIII of England accuses Luther of violating a nun sanctified by God, and of encouraging others to do the same. In the neighboring principality of Saxony, Duke Georg the Bearded reproaches Luther for allowing, as he says, the thorn of the flesh to tempt him, a beautiful Eve to seduce him. He supposedly chased the monks out of his cloister just so he and his Katharina could indulge their carnal lusts there undisturbed. No less grotesque are the defamations and accusations raised by the bishops and from the papal seat in Rome, which is overrun with illegitimate children and concubines. Luther is infuriated again and again by all this phony piety:

> For they know quite well that they could never find enough hog fixers to castrate all the priests. It's no secret that there are few priests who could lead chaste lives without being castrated, no matter how much they would like to. The bishops and canons make these demands, although they know that they cannot be carried out. And they themselves will not stop their disgraceful whoring. They are the biggest whore chasers of all. There's no need to cite witnesses: they do it brazenly for all to see, and yet they would force other people to practice chastity . . .

✦　✦　✦

Katharina isn't quite so sure what (besides being angry) really goes on inside Luther. She is his wife, there's no doubt about that. For exactly ten days now they have lived together in the Black Cloister. They are together, but there is a lot of space between them. She passes Luther the cup of wine, but he does not look her in the eye. She hands him the bread and he thanks her, but does not look up.

Is it because of the nights, when he does embrace her? If that's it, she'd gladly pack them off to Hell. She would prefer Luther to have back the calm, friendly manner he used to show her. His thoughtfulness when he tried to help with her unhappy romance.

Hieronymus. Has she forgotten him? Katharina Melanchthon reported recently that Baumgärtner is engaged to a sixteen-year-old girl from a wealthy burgher family in Bavaria. "I wish him God's blessing," Katharina said calmly. And her heartbeat remained perfectly steady.

Her husband, Martinus Luther, occupies Katharina entirely. She has a rough idea of why he is so self-conscious. They both know from long years in the cloister that pleasure—wild, wicked desire—proves the existence of original sin. The flesh does not obey the will. After baptism, wicked desire does stop being a sin, but it doesn't disappear. It was a torment even for the old church fathers. Katharina reads in a book that she finds in Martinus's room: Augustine complained constantly about nightly temptations, which he called pollutions. St. Jerome pounded his breast with a stone, so vehement were his temptations, but it didn't help. He could not control the evil, for he was unable to forget the maidens he had seen dancing in Rome. Francis, the barefooted monk, made snowballs and hugged and kissed them so that his wicked lust might pass. Benedict lay down naked among thorns and let them scratch him in order to rid himself of wicked lust. St. Bernard chastised himself and made his body tired and spent . . .

Katharina never suppressed her lust. In her childhood, she always liked exchanging caresses with Clara, and later with Ave. And with Hieronymus she would gladly have climbed into a bed. Thank heaven, there was none available. The threats of the older nuns that weighed so heavily on the minds of many novices (they were constantly accusing the younger ones of unchastity) Katharina never accepted. Nor did Ave. They listened to these tongue-lashings, only to laugh about them at night in their cells.

But Luther? Even from the pulpit he prays that God—"You who see through our fingers and make allowances for our weaknesses"— may sustain him in the holy state of matrimony.

Katharina resolves not to think about it any longer. Why should she go taking measurements in Luther's soul with a plumb line? She wouldn't find the truth anyway.

✦   ✦   ✦

Katharina sets about writing a letter to her Aunt Lene at Cloister Marienthron:

Grace and peace, dear Aunt Lene,

I am writing you today as Katharina Lutherin, for on June thirteenth, as you know, I became a married woman. Since then I have been feeling lonely, although I am living with three gentlemen here in the Black Cloister. One is my husband, the second Brisger, his former prior (who also plans to marry soon). The third is Wolf Sieberger, the famulus. Shouldn't I have a second woman here by my side? And of all people, you who delight so in breaking the rules, how could you find anything more against the rules than my marriage? Not in the Electorate of

Saxony, in Saxony, in all Germany, nor even in England or Rome will you find anything that breaks the rules like this.

Ask God and the Holy Virgin. I believe that what Luther says is true, namely that we attain grace better by means of service to our neighbor and by the simple fulfillment of our duties than we do by fasting and observing all the church's ceremonies. And you can fulfill your duties as infirmary mistress just by attending to Luther.

Now I will wait patiently while your heart decides.

Posted in Wittenberg on June 23, 1525

Katharina Lutherin

✦　✦　✦

June 27, 1525

Katharina and Luther's official wedding day, which according to custom always takes place some time after the consummation. It is evening and still warm. Katharina is sitting in the cloister garden and trying to think about nothing. This day, the splendid ceremony, has tired her. Luther comes and sits down beside her. They sit in silence, each absorbed in their own thoughts; suddenly they hear nightingales, and frogs in the Elbe meadows. "That's how it is in the world, too," says Luther abruptly, "the frogs drown out the nightingales, and the voice of Christ is drowned out by the shouting of Dr. Eck and Cochlaeus." Luther breaks off a carnation and smells it. This gesture reminds Katharina of another occasion when he smelled a carnation. It was during the summer six years ago, when he was at the Pleissenburg in Leipzig debating Dr. Eck, the theologian from Ingolstadt. This apparent disinterest on Luther's part left the whole world feeling insecure. Here his issues hang in the balance, so they said, and he is sniffing flowers . . .

Eck had the assignment from Rome to refute Luther's theses and writings on the basis of Holy Scripture. It was to be a scholarly debate, yet Eck was interested only in making a name for himself. Luther called the Pope the Antichrist, and the Romans heretics and pack animals who had reduced the sacrament to a gaudy public display, liquor sales, and money transactions.

Luther is still sniffing his carnation. His voice sounds bitter as he recalls: "In Leipzig, we were treated as enemies. They courted Eck, they had a robe of honor made for him and a silk camlet. Duke Georg of Saxony gave him a fat buck. And the disputation went the same way. Eck always had the last word. I wasn't allowed to defend myself."

Katharina knows that this thorn is still lodged in Luther's flesh. When he speaks of Dr. Eck, he usually calls him Dr. Sow.

Katharina likes listening to Luther. When he speaks, the images come to life before her eyes. She sees the fat Dominican, Tetzel, traveling throughout the land with pomp and circumstance, accompanied by a cardinal. Everywhere they set out a trunk with heavy iron fittings for the offerings, everywhere they post placards with a schedule of rates for the indulgences. Princes and heads of state pay twenty-five gulden, prelates and barons ten, better-situated burghers six, lesser burghers one, right down to the very poor, who can get theirs for just a half or even a quarter gulden. Women can even purchase an indulgence against the will of their husbands. They race madly to the indulgence vendors. "Even if you [this is what Tetzel called out to the people], even if you had got the Mother of God pregnant, I have such grace from the Pope that I can forgive you, provided you put the right amount of money into the box. When in my trunk the silver rings, the soul from Purgatory springs."

Money, money, money. Until now, Katharina hasn't had to worry about money. Never in the cloister, of course, and not in the Cranach house either, where she used to take Barbara's alms sack to market. She paid for her purchases from it and still had some left over to give to the poor! But now, now money worries confront her at every turn. Once she saw the spices, the fine linen, the fabric, the pots, the pheasants, chickens, cherries, and apples and took whatever was needed for the Cranach household. Today she goes to market, and behind every bird, every delicacy, behind every bolt of fabric she sees the gulden, groschen, and pfennige that it costs. Mostly she has only pfennige, and they are too few, so she comes home from market with her basket half full. And everything that urgently needs doing around the cloister costs money. Money that's not there. But there are people who have money, lots of money even. The princes, the patricians, the wealthy merchants like the Fuggers and Welsers in Augsburg, the Pirckheimers and Baumgärtners in Nuremberg. Yes, for Hieronymus, too, money was more important than his love for Katharina. Money is the god for which they'll sell out even

their God in Heaven. The greedy Popes in Rome—
Katharina can't even keep them apart, Leo the Medici,
then Hadrian, who ruled for just one year, and now there's
another Medici in the Holy See, an illegitimate one, but
he's Leo's cousin. He's named Clement VII. One thing they
have in common: They don't seek God, they seek power.
And power is money.

For the first few months, there was money in the Luther
house. The wedding brought it in. Elector Johann, who
succeeded his brother Friedrich onto the throne, gave
them a hundred gulden to set up housekeeping. And now
Luther earns a salary of one hundred gulden a year. The
new elector favors Luther, perhaps even more than the old
one did. Along with the unexpected monetary blessing, it
rained beer brewed in Einbeck and Torgau. The council
sent that, and wines from Franconia and the Moselle as
well. One week before the wedding ceremony, Katharina
went to the town hall and asked the council for Swabian
linen to make a wedding dress. A shower of sparks from the
hearth fire had fallen onto her holiday dress (she showed it
to them), and in the last rain mud from the streets had
ruined it completely.

And my husband, Katharina declared to the astonished
councillors, my husband has need of a new robe. Everything was delivered three days later. The finest linen for
Katharina, a purple robe with a black linen lining for
Professor Luther.

And then Luther's parents came to the wedding. They're
humble folk: the mother shy, the father dignified.

Katharina knows their discipline of Luther was harsh.

But it seems they also implanted in him that irrepressible drive to seek the truth. Or did God do that, and they were his tools? In any case, therein lies the honor that they deserve and the reward that they need, now that they are in the winter of their lives.

The solitude in Katharina's soul suddenly awakens a great desire within her: she wants Luther's parents to love her. The couple, who have come and greeted her so openly, have touched Katharina profoundly. She hurries here and there, fetches comfortable cushions, rubs the forehead of Frau Luther, who suffers from severe headaches, with an ointment made from oils of chamomile, dill, and rue, to which she has added ground pepper. The treatment helps. Margarete Luther is surprised and relieved.

The old couple walk with dignity behind the bride and groom in the wedding procession.

The church is full. Everyone wants to see the great Dr. Luther be married. Elisabeth Cruziger, like Katharina a former nun, and now married to Professor Kaspar Cruziger, has taught the children's choir a song:

> Lord Jesus, only son of God
> Of the eternal Father
> Sprung from his very heart
> Just as it is written
> He is the morning star
> His radiance shines far
> Of all the stars the clearest.

✦　✦　✦

As they leave the church, a woman breaks out of the crowd of onlookers—it's Klara, the wife of Lorenz Jessner. She spits at Katharina and Luther and shouts curses at them. Walpurga Bugenhagen, who steps in front of Katharina to keep her attacker at a distance, gets kicked and shoved; finally, the furious woman is led away.

Much sweetness, much sorrow. Katharina is tired. The old Luthers are already asleep. It does Katharina good to exchange such heartfelt warmth with the two of them. Luther is and remains reserved, distant. In his letter to Nikolas Amsdorf—Katharina saw it by coincidence—he wrote: "I love and esteem my Katharina."

What exactly is "love and esteem"?

With a sigh, she stands up. Luther, who has been sitting in silence the whole time, rises as well. He puts his arm around Katharina, draws her to him. He quotes from Elisabeth Cruziger's song: "He is the morning star, His radiance shines far, Of all the stars the clearest . . .

"You, Katharina, are my morning star."

For the first time since the wedding, his eyes meet hers.

5

JUNE 7, 1526

Beneath the warm June sun, the Wittenberg market square is full of activity. A troupe of itinerant actors has set up a plank stage. More and more people come running to see the show. Curious, Katharina moves closer. She has never seen such a performance.

Three characters appear on stage: Pope Julius II with his triple tiara and magnificent robe; his *Genius*, or guardian angel, in a white tunic; and St. Peter (looking through a window in a set depicting the gates of Haven).

Katharina knows that there was unspeakable debauchery and whoring in Rome under Pope Julius between 1503 and 1513. Luther told her about it—one of the many times he began fuming about the papists. He said, "If Hell is an actual place, then I believe Rome stands on it."

> *Julius:* (shouts) What sort of foolishness is this? Can't the gate be opened?
> *Genius:* You'd better make sure you're using the right key. You don't open this gate with the key to the strongbox.
> *Julius:* (shouts even louder) But I've never owned any key besides this one!

Genius: Actually, neither have I. Well, we're locked out for now.

Julius: That makes my bile boil! I'm going to knock at this gate. Hey! Hey in there! Open this door right now! Why is the gatekeeper so lazy? He's snoring, I think, and he's utterly drunk!

Genius: (to the audience) How he keeps expecting everyone else to be like him . . .

St. Peter: It's a good thing our heavenly gates are made of iron, or that fellow out there would have knocked them down. He must be some sort of giant, a destroyer of cities. But, immortal God, what's that stench I smell? I'd better just look out this window first . . . Who are you, and what do you want?

Julius: Hey you, get that gate open—all the way open. People like me you should come out and meet, and bring all your heavenly hosts with you.

St. Peter: First explain to me who you are.

Julius: As if you couldn't see that for yourself!

St. Peter: I should be able to tell by looking at you? I do see a new creature I've never seen before—that is to say, a monster.

Julius: If you're not completely blind, do you at least recognize this golden key, the threefold crown, and the coat studded with gold and precious stones?

St. Peter: That key? Well, it is certainly very different from the one given me by Christ, the true shepherd of the church.

Julius: Let's cut out the childish silliness now. In case you don't know it, I am the famous Julius from Liguria, and you recognize no doubt the two letters here, P.M., assuming you ever learned your alphabet.

St. Peter: They mean, I believe, *Pestis Maximus,* greatest plague.

Genius: (aside) Well, this clairvoyant was right on target that time . . .

Julius: (screaming) No, they stand for *Pontifex Maximus,* highest priest . . .

✦   ✦   ✦

The audience howls and doubles over with laughter. Katharina would like to stay and listen, but she has sharp pains in her back. She is pregnant. The child isn't due for another three weeks, but her lower back hurts so badly she can hardly stand. For a moment, the marketplace swims before her eyes. She sits down on a grain sack. A market woman smiles knowingly and hands her a leather water bottle.

Cautiously Katharina gets back to her feet and starts on her way home. Her joy is suddenly replaced by great fear. The verse from Isaiah (14:12) occurs to her: "How you have fallen from Heaven, you who shone this morning!"

Lately this can happen to Katharina at any moment. In the morning she is looking forward to her child, seeing everything in a bright light, then suddenly she is depressed, plagued with fears. Child of a nun, of a monk. From the union of monk and nun comes the Antichrist.

Again and again these slanderous words are directed at Katharina. Now in the alleyway, now in the church. They are like pinpricks by day and millstones by night. Then sometimes they rise up and frighten her so badly that she breaks out in a sweat. She sees Barbara's dead little daughter, that striking round head in its waxen stillness. The linen weaver's youngest died. The wife of Rump, the blacksmith, had a child that wouldn't come out. So they both died, Rumpin and the child . . .

Then Katharina gets up silently and goes to see Aunt Lene, who has been living with them since Christmas. She was only too glad to respond to Katharina's request that she come. Meanwhile, the whole of Cloister Marienthron has become Lutheran. Aunt Lene comforts Katharina, and usually she strains her a cup of red wine with cloves, cinnamon, nutmeg, and honey. That soothes the nerves and drives away the melancholy.

Every day Katharina is reminded afresh how glad she is to have her aunt here.

Today is no exception. When Aunt Lene sees Katharina, her gruff expression returns: "I don't know much about women going into labor, but I think I'd better get towels and some water ready."

Katharina is beginning to think so, too. She sends Wolf after Sandnerin, the midwife.

But the pains in her lower back disappear again. Katharina sets the table in the main room, as she does every noon. No longer is it just Luther, Brisger, and Wolf who eat with her. Besides Aunt Lene, there are four students and the scribes who live in the house. Also, Spalatin has come over from Altenburg for a few days. He is married and reports that he and his wife are also eagerly awaiting the arrival of a child.

Luther speaks at table of nothing but the impending

birth. He is constantly urging Katharina to lie down and rest. But she would rather be moving about. And that is what she does, even though she knows that Luther doesn't take it well when she disobeys his advice.

◆　◆　◆

When Luther found out that Katharina had made demands of the council in Wittenberg, the two of them had their first quarrel. He accused her of disobedience, and she shot back: "Why am I disobedient when I don't want the two of us wearing tattered clothes to our wedding?"

"You should have asked me first!"

"But you never have time. You always have Jonas and Melanchthon and Schlaginhaufen and the famulus and Lord knows who else with you . . . Besides, when it comes to money you let people walk all over you."

Now Luther is shouting. "Was it the hangman that brought me this wife?"

In the kitchen, Katharina furiously clatters pots and saucepans. The Devil take it! The little money that they have Luther passes out with both hands. It is common knowledge that no one who knocks at the door of the Black Cloister goes away empty-handed. Word of such things gets around. The printers Lotter, Lufft, and Schirlentz each wanted to give Luther four hundred gulden a year for the publication of his writings. They certainly have grown rich enough on them. But Luther refused. Refused! Nor does he take fees for his lectures. Actually, Melanchthon doesn't take any either. But he and his wife both have wealthy parents who are often giving them money. At the Luther house it's different; the iron chest is always empty, because the master of the house keeps giving its contents to the poor. And the water pipes that Katharina wants so badly have not been laid yet, and the baking oven has not been built yet, and the bathing room still has no tiles and no drainage pit.

But then Katharina again sees how Luther is suffering from the devastating effects of the peasants' revolt. How daily his remorse grows over writing *Against the Thieving and Murdering Hordes of Peasants.* Now he is drawing up an *Epistle Against the Pamphlet Against the Peasants.*

In her heart, Katharina is all for the peasants. Once she says as much to Luther. He stares at her in silence and walks away.

That evening, the discord climbs with them into bed; Luther rolls onto his side without a word. Katharina sees his powerful, naked back. She is suddenly moved to touch him. Her anger is long since gone. And so she playfully begins counting his vertebrae. That turns into a caressing. Luther doesn't move. Then she snuggles right up to him and reaches her arms around him. Nothing. Katharina sobs a little now. That comes to her easily, but she herself is touched by the presence of these unusually tender feelings. She sobs, "Martinus, Martinus." And—finally—Martinus turns toward her. A relaxed giggling and snuggling begins and for the first time becomes lovemaking. It is a having and giving, a lifting up and falling back into luminous depths, a grappling for more, ever more.

✦   ✦   ✦

From then on, this strong nocturnal flame burns for them often. But that makes it all the harder for Katharina by day to endure the undemonstrative, impatient, constantly over-worked Martinus. Why can't he carry over something from the nights into the days? By day he is the professor, the preacher, the reformer, the monk. He demands obedience from everyone—and everyone complies. Even Aunt Lene.

In the meanwhile, the midwife has arrived. She examines Katharina and says it's time to get started. Now Martinus insists that Katharina get into bed. In the end, she obeys, although she would rather be in the kitchen with Aunt Lene distilling medicinal potions and preparing ointments. After only a short time in Wittenberg, Aunt Lene has acquired a reputation for her knowledge of the healing arts. Even the apothecary from Cranach's shop talks herbs and potions with her.

And an herb for birthing? The pains are getting stronger now. From the main room she hears Martinus speaking to all assembled at table. She can't understand everything, but individual sentences and scraps of sentences make it clear that the topic is still woman and the ordeal she must endure. Why doesn't Martinus come to her? Why doesn't he sit down by her bed?

Instead, she hears him outside: "When a woman is about to give birth, she lives in fear—just as you live in fear when the cross and its suffering overtake you. The midwife and others who are there may offer comfort, but they cannot put off the ordeal. The woman must go through it and risk her life."

Katharina is furious when she hears this. It's easy for him to preach about it. Let the Devil come take her pain and give it to Martinus.

Katharina knows she's being unfair. She senses that

Martinus is talking so much only because he is afraid himself. She hears his voice: "And really, no one can help her. She must go through it."

Holy Mother of God, yes, I have to go through it.

Toward midnight, the child is born. The midwife cuts the umbilical cord and ties it with a fine linen thread. Katharina watches little Johannes being bathed. The midwife drizzles olive oil into his eyes and wraps him securely in linen cloths. Then she gives the child to Martinus, who stands silently looking at it.

Lucas and Barbara Cranach come; Lucas is Hänschen's godfather.

Katharina wants to sleep, just sleep. But the others are so busy, so excited, that she tries not to sleep after all.

Even Wolf Sieberger has gotten up. And he doesn't leave his bed even when there's a storm. Now he comes and lays a pinwheel, a top, and a clapper beside the baby. He made them himself. Out of love. Lucas Cranach pulls out a bossed cup of gold and silver. Now we're just one short of the three wise men, Katharina thinks sleepily. And sure enough, here comes Melanchthon, a bit hesitantly.

Impulsively, Katharina holds out both arms to him. "It's been a long time since we danced together."

"Yes, Katharina, far too long," says Melanchthon, and he presses her gently to him for a moment. Luther embraces him.

The child is sleeping now, after whimpering for a while. Everyone looks at his little head. A healthy child, God be praised.

Martinus gives the cradle a gentle push. It sounds sad but defiant when he says, "Enemy to this child and to all that is mine are the Pope, Duke Georg, and all those who side with the Pope. Also all the devils. The child does not worry about these things. God be praised. He is not afraid, and does not ask why there are so many powerful men who wish him ill."

"But there are also many who stand by you." Melanchthon says this. His young, sensitive scholar's face, which so often looks unhappy and tormented, is relaxed. And that's not only because of the soft light from the tallow lamps. Katharina knows that Melanchthon has been suffering because he was among the early opponents of her marriage to Martinus. He didn't go out and shout it like the others did, but he did write to his friend, Camerarius, in Leipzig, "The nuns, who are knowledgeable in all craft, have got him on a string . . ."

Katharina knows who whispered that into his ear. His wife. She has never forgiven Katharina that Melanchthon made friends with her so readily, that he danced with her happily and playfully. And today she does not forgive Katharina for becoming heartfelt friends with Katharina Jonas, with Walpurga Bugenhagen, with Elisabeth Cruziger, and not least of all with Barbara Cranach. And she is also envious that Lutherin is of the nobility, and married to someone who, as Doctor and reformer, ranks ahead of Melanchthon, whose title is Magister.

Katharina believes she knows what thoughts are concealed behind Melanchthon's high, pale forehead. But one thing she does not understand. Why does the extremely intelligent and learned Melanchthon clearly let his wife direct him in so many things? Why hasn't he yet dared to come to Luther's house and speak openly about his views? Every time he has been there, he has just discussed business with Luther and then left hurriedly. As if he were fleeing.

It also puzzles Katharina that Melanchthon treats his wife with such affection and courtesy. She has often noticed this in church or at other gatherings. While his wife (who is known for her brusque demeanor) makes a sour face and stares at the floor, Melanchthon speaks to her amicably and holds her solicitously by the arm.

Martinus is far removed from such demonstrations of affection. When did he ever escort Katharina up the stairs? Not even when she was very pregnant. When does he turn to Katharina in conversation? It is always she who asks him a question, makes a request. The other day, he again brought her up short when she called the elector's chancellor, Brück, an ass because he won't approve having a cellar dug beneath the Black Cloister. "Curb your quick tongue," Luther said. (Although he knows perfectly well that Brück really is an ass.)

Once, Katharina complains to Barbara Cranach about Luther's lack of attentiveness.

"Well," Barbara says calmly, "don't forget that he was a monk for forty-two years."

That makes sense to Katharina. Luther does have something of the monk about him. Fortunately, only by day.

✦　✦　✦

Barbara lends Katharina a book that she received from Lucas at Christmas. It is bound in leather and decorated with an engraving in red and gold. The title: *How a Wife*

Should Make Her Husband Friendly. The author is Erasmus of Rotterdam.

Katharina reads:

Eulalia: Good day, my dear Xanthippe. I am very glad to see you.

Xanthippe: The pleasure's all mine, my good Eulalia. Why, you've grown even prettier than you were.

Eulalia: And you're still the same old mockingbird.

Xanthippe: No, not at all, it really seems so to me.

Eulalia: Maybe my new dress looks particularly well on me.

Xanthippe: You're right. It's been a long time since I've seen anything as elegant. It strikes me as English cloth.

Eulalia: English cloth dyed in Venice.

Xanthippe: It feels softer than silk. What charming purple and red! Where did you get this magnificent gift?

Eulalia: Who else do virtuous wives receive gifts from but their husbands?

Xanthippe: You certainly did find a good match in your marriage. And I married such a drip when I fell for my Klaus.

Eulalia: That's the first I've heard of it! Has something gone amiss between you?

Xanthippe: I'll never be content with him. Just look what a rag I'm wearing. This is how he lets his wife run around. I'm so ashamed I want to hide whenever I cross the street and see how other women are dressed, women who, God knows, made worse matches than I did.

Eulalia: The adornment of a virtuous woman lies not in her clothing and outward appearance, as the Apostle Peter says [cf. I Peter 3:3] —I heard that recently in a sermon—but rather in chaste and virtuous manners and in the nobility of her spirit. Prostitutes make a point of drawing all eyes to themselves; it must suffice for us to please our husbands alone.

Xanthippe: Meanwhile, this good man, who keeps his wife on such a tight budget, is spending his way through my dowry, and it was certainly not a small sum that I brought to this marriage.

Eulalia: How?

Xanthippe: However he pleases: with drinking, debauchery, and dice.

Eulalia: You don't say!

Xanthippe: Sad but true. Late at night, when I have waited long enough for him, he comes home drunk, snores all night and vomits all over the bed, and that's only part of it.

Eulalia: Stop, stop! When you make your husband look bad, you're making yourself look bad.

Xanthippe: May I fall down dead if I wouldn't rather lie with a pig than with such a man!

Eulalia: And don't you receive him with scolding and carping?

Xanthippe: Just as he deserves! So he knows that I'm not mute.

Eulalia: And what does he do then?

Xanthippe: At first he let loose too, thinking he could impress me with his shouting.

Eulalia: Was shouting all that happened? Weren't there blows delivered as well?

Xanthippe: Only once did the quarreling become so heated that we nearly went at each other.

Eulalia: Oh, that's frightful!

Xanthippe: He had already raised his club, roared like a bull, and threatened me.

Eulalia: Didn't your heart just sink?

Xanthippe: Not a chance! I grabbed a chair, and if he had so much as touched me with his little finger, he would have found out that I have hands, too.

Eulalia: That's a new kind of shield! All you'd need is a distaff as a lance.

Xanthippe: He surely would have learned what sort of a woman he's dealing with.

Eulalia: Listen, my dear Xanthippe, that's not right.

Xanthippe: What's not right? If he doesn't treat me like a wife, I don't have to treat him as my husband.

Eulalia: But St. Paul said wives should be subject to their husbands in all virtue and honor [Ephesians 5:24]. And Peter holds up the example of Sarah, who called her husband, Abraham, her lord [I Peter 3:6].

Xanthippe: That's nothing new to me. But the same Paul also says that husbands should love their wives as Christ loves his bride, the Church [Ephesians 5:25]. Let Klaus be mindful of his duty, and I will do the same.

Eulalia: But once things have reached the point where one or the other must yield, then it is right that the wife yield to the husband.

Xanthippe: Can he be called a husband, when he treats me like a maidservant?

Eulalia: But tell me, dearest Xanthippe, did he quit threatening you with his fists?

Xanthippe: He was smart enough to stop that, or he would have been the one to get a beating.

Eulalia: But you didn't stop carping and scolding?

Xanthippe: No, and I don't intend to stop.

Eulalia: And what does he do then?

Xanthippe: What does he do? Sometimes he acts as if he's sleeping, once in a while he gets laughing and doesn't stop, and sometimes he takes his lute, which barely has three strings left, and plays it as loud as he can to drown out my scolding.

Eulalia: And that really gets you mad?

Xanthippe: I can't even tell you how mad it gets me! Sometimes I find it hard not to just start pounding him with my fists.

Eulalia: Dear Xanthippe, may I speak openly with you?

Xanthippe: Why not?

Eulalia's advice tends toward the wife's needing to be constantly gracious and serene, always attentive to the moods and whims of her spouse, always calming and soothing him. She may never be jovial when her husband is ill-tempered. Not cheerful when he is upset. When he has drunk a glass more than thirst requires, she should treat him even more graciously, and accompany him to bed with good words.

Katharina is completely on the side of Xanthippe, who says in the book: "How miserable is the lot of a wife if she is supposed to accept everything in silence, no matter whether her husband is drunk or otherwise does whatever he pleases."

Barbara, on the other hand, thinks Eulalia is very much the wiser one. She herself would agree with her for the most part. Especially when Eulalia says: "How stupid it would be of us to respond in kind. After all, our men have to endure our moods, too. Besides, there are times when a woman can influence her husband on important matters. So in lesser things it's smarter to give some ground."

"I'm not so sure," says Katharina, as she reads passages in the book again and again. "Don't you think it's wrong to conceal one's true thoughts just to keep your husband happy?"

Barbara thinks awhile. Then she sighs. "Oh, I think sometimes it actually is the smarter thing to do. What good does it do to poison your days with quarreling? They are hard enough as it is."

✦   ✦   ✦

In the past few months, Barbara has been depressed more and more often. Sometimes, when Katharina comes by, her friend will be sitting idle, gazing out the window. Or she will be looking at her hands.

"Melancholicus," says Dr. Schurf. "Avoid all heavy foods." Barbara should eat only tender meat, preferably young pigeon, chicken, or fish from flowing water. Better to steam them with parsley and vinegar than to fry them. Again today, Katharina has brought herbs from Aunt Lene that should cheer her up: watercress, sage, hyssop, fennel, and endive greens.

Cranach says to Katharina, "Please, come as often as you can."

Katharina's free time keeps shrinking. Little Hans is now a year old. He can't walk yet, but he's a great crawler. Katharina, Aunt Lene, and Lisbeth, the maid, can't watch him enough. Above all, the open hearth fire holds a powerful attraction for him. Whenever flying sparks land on him or he has burned himself on the hot stones, he screams so loudly that Luther comes racing from his tower study. "In the name of Christ, can't three women manage to watch my little son?"

Most of the time, Wolf Sieberger takes the little fellow down to the garden. Soon after the wedding, Katharina saw to it that a new well was drilled there, so that the whole untended area could be thoroughly watered. The well, this first major construction project of Katharina's, which plunged the Luther household into debt for a long time (all told, it cost one hundred gulden), led again to discord between husband and wife. Luther had wanted to wait before starting the work, and Katharina finally called in the workers without his consent.

She replies to his angry reproaches that she is tired of spending money for every bunch of parsley, for every pea and bean, for every carrot and every head of lettuce. "At the market, things are getting more expensive by the day, and we have more and more mouths to feed. You tell me how I'm to pay for everything." When Luther remarks ironically that she could go to market many times for a hundred gulden, she shoots back: "Yes, I could, if you hadn't given it all the day before to some loafer."

Luther shouts in return: "A man would be better off

dead than to have such a devil for a wife!"

He stands before her, his face white with rage. Then he turns around and leaves. His eyes really can blaze, thinks Katharina. It crosses her mind that Cajetan called Luther "that beast." Katharina reasons that Martinus only yells when people attack him, when they attack him wrongly. And she, Katharina, has just now behaved toward him as an enemy. Why did she act behind his back? And why, when he rightly complained about it, did she scold him about his generosity?

Immediately Katharina follows Martinus to his workroom. She asks the scribe to leave her alone with her husband for a moment. As Martinus stays seated at his table and doesn't move, she reaches her arms around his neck from behind. "Martin, please forgive me. The Devil must have gotten into me. I'm so sorry that I offended you."

Martinus pushes her away, then looks at her, somewhat placated. "No one is so wicked that they don't have at least one quality that deserves praise. Not even you."

This encounter runs through Katharina's mind for a long while. One thought won't let her go: that Eulalia played some part in her, Katharina's, quickness to apologize to Martinus. That would be strange enough in itself. For it would mean that Erasmus of Rotterdam—Martinus's greatest opponent, of all people—had become the peacemaker between of them. She can't get that thought out of her head. She'd love to tell Martinus, but she knows better than to try.

✦   ✦   ✦

Martinus views Erasmus of Rotterdam with enmity. Katharina sees the matter differently. Erasmus did slander her before her wedding to Luther, but Katharina forgave him after he apologized in writing for doing so—and said she was gracious as well. She also found out that the traveling actors' play about Pope Julius was written by Erasmus. She is more and more delighted with the dialogue between Eulalia and Xanthippe each time she reads it. Erasmus, Katharina is sure, is someone who understands people. Even if he doesn't necessarily love them.

From conversations among Luther, Melanchthon, and Schlaginhaufen, Katharina has learned that the famed Erasmus (whom Melanchthon admires, much to Luther's chagrin), this adviser to kings and popes, now sits hesitant and undecided between two stools. The Lutherans consider him a papist, the Catholics of the old faith think he's a Lutheran. He's in danger of losing everyone's sympathies. So he has staked out his position in a tract titled *On Free Will*. In it, Erasmus poses the question of the magnitude of God and the magnitude of man. He assumes that man can educate himself, develop, form himself into a person. However, this position in favor of the free will of man is seen as a limitation on the magnitude and omnipotence of God. Martinus has explained this to his wife, who has read the tract again and again. And he adds: "That is heretical. In another age he would have been burned at the stake."

Katharina, upset that Martinus is refuting the great Erasmus, says heatedly, "But why don't you answer him, why do you let that stand? It is your duty to all Christians

not to let that stand!" Finally she has persuaded Luther to
act. In December he writes to Erasmus:

> The Holy Spirit is no skeptic, and what it has
> written in our hearts is not in doubt and not mere
> opinions, but rather binding assertions that are
> surer and more solid than life itself and all our
> experience.

✦　✦　✦

The summer of 1527 is hot and dry. The earth seems to
split open beneath the heat. Once in a while there is lightning that brings no rain, just burning barns here and there.
A black multitude of wildly shrieking rooks flies over the
Elbe. Katharina, Wolf Sieberger, and the maids work in the
garden and in the grain field that Katharina has leased. The
work seems to get harder by the day. They'll need to harvest everything; the fruits have to be dried for the winter
or boiled in honey syrup. But they all like working in the
garden and the field. Even the dinner guests help. For the
house is not a good place to be. For weeks and months
Luther has been entangled in a dispute over the Eucharist.
His rage against the Swiss and the Swabians sits with them
at table and goes with them to bed. The primary dispute is
over the doctrine of the Eucharist. On the one hand,
Zwingli, Oecolampadius, Butzer, and Capito support a
symbolic understanding of the Eucharist: bread and wine
signify the body and blood of Christ. Luther, on the other
hand, firmly insists upon the version that the bread and
wine *are* the body and blood of Christ.

Besides this dispute, which requires much time and

energy, Martinus is still fully engaged in building up his new church in the Electorate of Saxony. He makes official visits, cautiously institutes regulations and procedures for the congregations, and brings his music into the churches.

Now the Black Cloister sometimes serves as a cantoria as well. Martinus has brought to Wittenberg the singer and choirmaster Johann Walther from Torgau, and the musician Rupff. A cantor from Leipzig who has set up a music press in Wittenberg publishes the songs. The type is cut in Lucas Cranach's workshop. Late into the night they sit at the table with quill and note paper. Martinus paces back and forth through the room, humming and occasionally sounding out a tune on the flute. Katharina knows that Martinus loves music above all else and is often quite sad that he no longer has the time to compose or to write lyrics or even to play the flute or the lute himself.

Once he says, "The Devil need not have all the lovely tunes."

Katharina alone knows that Luther is hopelessly overworking himself. People are constantly in his workroom: the couriers from the printer, his colleagues Bugenhagen, Jonas, and Cruziger . . . or Rörer, who reads proof. Martinus is always dictating, writing on his own, disputing, listening to petitioners, mediating arguments—as Katharina sees it, the Black Cloister is often like a madhouse. Not even at table is there a measure of peace. Especially Martinus spoons his food quickly, heedlessly. There's always disputing, disputing . . .

"Tomorrow we'll serve them sawdust," she tells Aunt Lene once in the kitchen.

At night, in his few hours of sleep, the Devil takes

revenge. The demons overtake him: "You are not God, you're the Devil himself!" Martinus shouts once. "No escape, no comfort. Accusation and damnation. The soul is stretched on the cross of Christ, you can count all its bones. Everything is fulfilled with awful bitterness, with terror, with fear, with sadness—and all this without end, eternally."

Martinus is shouting so loudly in his dream that Katharina tries to wake him. She shakes his shoulders, slaps his cheeks, and finally he comes to. Katharina sends Wolf to get Bugenhagen. Only then does she light the three candles on the ledge.

She stares fearfully at Martinus. He tosses and turns, moans, is soaked with sweat.

"Martinus, tell me, what's wrong?"

With his fever, his nightmares and fears, the sick man is unable to speak.

Aunt Lene has awakened; she arrives with warm towels and begins giving Martinus a rubdown. Katharina massages his forehead with a salve.

Then Martinus says softly, "Bugenhagen. I want to make my confession."

She tells him that she has already sent for Bugenhagen.

Katharina can scarcely keep her horror to herself. Why does Martinus want to make a confession? Why is he so afraid? Now he begins again screaming with pain, then whimpering as he writhes in the bed . . .

Holy Mother of God. Katharina is glad when Bugenhagen comes. It is as if the peace of God were entering the room along with his large, heavy frame. He is able to calm Martin.

They all sit around Martin's bed. Katharina clasps his hand tightly. "Martin," she implores him silently, "stomp around the house again, shout at us, call us brides of Satan, scold, do what you want, but get back up, be the old Martinus again!"

Suddenly he screams: "The pot, the pot!"

After he has urinated, Katharina finds blood and a stone the size of a lentil. Martinus loses consciousness. Is he dying?

"I'll fetch Dr. Schurf!" Bugenhagen runs out:

Katharina prays, "To you I call, Lord, my rock, do not turn silently away from me. Hear my loud plea when I cry to you. The Lord is my strength and my shield, my heart trusts in him . . .

Finally, Martin is asleep.

Dr. Schurf and Aunt Lene are disputing in the kitchen. The doctor wants to put hot bricks into bed with his patient. Aunt Lene is absolutely opposed to the idea: "You can't put sick kidneys near fire. And they shouldn't be exposed to any other form of heat, either."

As for his diet, the two experts agree: don't overeat, don't drink too much, but don't fast too much or too long, either. Martinus should never go to sleep right after a meal. And he should never sleep lying on his back. That would put too much pressure on the kidneys, says Dr. Schurf. Also, the patient should eat no salted meat (or fish), no coarse meat from cow or pig, nor any venison. He should eat no birds that feed in the water. And no baked goods, especially not pies and pastries.

"Martinus, now we can't let you have any of the things you like to eat."

Yes. Also anger, hatred, and melancholy must be avoided. Gracious God, how will Martinus ever recover?

The next morning, Melanchthon arrives. He finds Martinus weak but pain-free. Melanchthon has news from Rome. Cardinal Pompeo Colonna and his troops entered Rome. Pope Clement had to flee to the Castel Sant' Angelo. Word is that Colonna's men plundered palaces, churches, even the Vatican.

Meanwhile, Colonna has been driven out, but now the mercenaries are carrying out a second *Sacco di Roma*—and this time on a grand scale. Left entirely to their own devices, the hordes run wild in the Eternal City. They go on plundering for months; they leave untouched only the banking house of the Fugger family, which transfers huge payments to them in Augsburg.

The German mercenaries have thought up a special pastime. One of their leaders, Wilhelm von Sandizell, dresses up with some of his band as a Roman pope, complete with triple tiara, and the others are decked out as cardinals. Then, in front of the Castel Sant' Angelo the "cardinals" kneel in obeisance to their "Pope." And at the end they shout out, "Let's make Luther the Pope. All in favor, raise your hands."

So they all raise their hands and shout, "Luther, Pope!"

The Germans and Spaniards are brawling in the streets, and both together against the Italians. St. Peter's is being plundered. The Spaniards are feared on account of their brutal rapes and tortures. It is said that they rape the Roman women and their daughters before the eyes of their husbands and fathers. They roast the soles of the men's feet in a fire and then hang them by their genitals.

The dead are left lying in the street. The city begins to stink, and there are outbreaks of the Roman fever, *terzana*. With the aid of the rotting corpses, these spread and join together, becoming an epidemic that carries the name of plague. The victors begin dying . . .

6

IT IS AUTUMN. Katharina walks through the garden and the fields to the meadows along the Elbe. She has little Hans by the hand; he can walk pretty well by now. It is early afternoon; the air has the stillness of midsummer and the sky is a precious blue, an almost dangerous blue for this time of year. An unaccustomed tiredness has come over Katharina. One that tells her she should stop pushing herself and get some rest, go for a walk with Hänschen. Katharina devotes far too little time to her son. She knows this, and she also knows why. She would need ten hands and ten brains and ten mouths to watch over the help, the animals, the workmen who constantly fill the Black Cloister with noisy activity that has already become infamous far and wide.

Poor Herr Doktor, people say. In his house there's such a motley crew of scholars, boys and girls, widows and children, that poor Dr. Luther never gets any peace.

"And me?" Katharina thinks, "do I get any peace?" Other than Aunt Lene, she didn't invite these guests into her home. And it's not her doing that their number keeps growing. Four orphaned children of Luther's sister they adopted. Katharina and Martinus were glad to have Endres and Cyriakus Kaufmann along with their sisters Else and Lene, especially since now little Hans will no longer be the only child toddling around among all these adults.

The dog, Tölpel, races around Katharina and Hänschen. Martin brought him into the house as a little puppy so that Hänschen could play with him. And play they do—Hänschen even likes to eat out of Tölpel's bowl. Now the boy is trudging along beside his mother. Katharina is happy that her Hans has strong little legs. He is a pretty child, they say he looks a lot like Katharina. But she sees Martinus in him, or his grandmother Margarete Luther. Back when they were putting baby bonnets on him, it often crossed Katharina's mind that the boy resembled Martin's mother.

Now they're passing a field where a peasant on horseback is slicing open the earth with a harrow. He has placed a large stone atop the harrow so that it penetrates deep enough into the soil. The peasant's wife, a seed pouch of white linen around her shoulder, broadcasts the seed. She is pregnant, evidently in about the same month as Katharina.

The son of the peasant couple, maybe five or six years old, is shooting a rough-hewn arrow with his bow. Rooks pick at the grain the peasant woman has cast onto the field. The woman sees Katharina and gives her a smile that is open and sisterly.

Katharina returns the smile. When someone shows her goodwill, it can make her happy for hours. In the alleys and in the villages she often has such encounters, though less often in Wittenberg, where gossip has drawn a definite picture of Katharina. *Proud* and *arrogant* they call her there.

Katharina is now in the meadows along the banks of the Elbe. Tired from the heat, she sits down in the parched grass, and Hänschen snuggles up next to her. Suddenly Katharina hears the clip-clop of horses' hooves, faintly at first, but coming closer. The sounds of talking and laughter emerge as well. Tölpel lifts his head and growls softly, but he stays by Katharina's side.

Up from their left comes a party on horseback. They must be from the duke's house—Katharina can tell instantly by their splendid clothes. The riders are wearing loose, embroidered coats. The first, obviously a young nobleman, is wearing all white beneath a red cape. Another appears entirely in azure blue except for the black biretta he is wearing despite (or on account of) the heat. The third horseman is attired in a splendid red; even his leggings are red, as are his biretta and the feathers in it.

Even more splendid are the young ladies, whom the gentlemen are now helping down from their saddles. The first and evidently the youngest of them is especially beautiful. Katharina sees a delicate face, light skin, the mouth very red, and the eyes dark. She is clad entirely in green. Three strings of pearls shimmer above a low-cut bodice. The very loose sleeves of her light dress are lined with azure blue dotted with golden stars. Resting atop her long curls is a schapel, the wreath of leaves or flowers that only young girls wear. This schapel is made of green leaves. Never before has Katharina seen such a beautiful, splendid girl. She is obviously the focal point of the party. The two other young women are also richly attired: with her light pink dress, the one wears a rosé-colored hat artfully perched atop dark hair and decorated with a brooch and pearls. The other has a blue dress richly embroidered with gold flowers. Over the blond hair that flows down one side of her head like a waterfall, she is wearing a schapel of flowers, probably rosé-colored roses.

The ducal party of six is not alone. Servants have come along. Maids spread out a great white cloth, they bring baskets of fruit and pitchers and cups. Laughter and chatter ensue; they play blindman's buff like children and dance together.

Katharina watches them as if under a spell. This visible ease of living, these colors, this joy, this luxury—she knows such things only from stories. Has she ever wished to live in such brilliant circumstances? Katharina looks at her hands. They are finely shaped, the nails have large half-moons. They could be beautiful. But the skin is rough in places, and the nails could use more regular care . . .

With a sigh, Katharina gets to her feet. Hänschen pulled away from her a while earlier and has run down closer to the Elbe. Now he is standing on the bank and pointing, while Tölpel barks wildly. When Katharina comes closer, she cries out in horror. Bloated, dead rats are lying there.

Katharina takes Hänschen by the hand and hurries away. One of the noblemen, hearing her cry, looks over toward the riverbank as well.

"Rats," he shouts to the others. "Lots of dead rats! They carry the plague!"

Looking back, Katharina sees the ducal party mount their horses and ride off.

✦   ✦   ✦

A few days later the plague bell sounds in Wittenberg. "The plague! The plague!" it clangs through the alleys, across the courtyards, along the stairways. People in the streets avoid each other. Contagion. Mothers anxiously feel their children's bodies. Are death-bringing knots forming in the groin, in the armpits? There is a horrific dying under way. In Magdeburg four hundred are already dead, in Leipzig six hundred, the same number in Erfurt. In Eisenach, a whole cloister died of the bubonic plague.

Death comes to all—the butcher, the cooper, the blacksmith, the apothecary, the doctor. Nobody can save him or herself. The plague casts its deadly shadow into the peasants' shacks and into the splendid houses and estates of the wealthy. Nor does it spare the aristocrats and the princes.

In the Black Cloister it first strikes Jost Honold, a young student from Augsburg who has been living with the Luther family for three months. Shivering with fever, the tall, handsome young man lies on his bed. Katharina and Aunt Lene attend to him in shifts. They wrap him in blankets, put hot tiles into bed with him so that he can sweat. When the buboes appear, so do the pain and the fear of death. Jost's beautiful, dark eyes are wide open. They follow Katharina with a mute question: Am I going to die? But I don't want to die!

Katharina washes him with a concentrated extract of ironweed and spleenwort. Aunt Lene prepares him the golden plague egg: a fresh egg is cracked open at the pointed end, the white removed and the shell filled with saffron. Then the egg is sealed and placed on hot stones to roast until the yolk is hard and the saffron completely dry. Added to that are white mustard seeds, tormentil, bistort, and camphor. All the ingredients are then ground together. If you have it, you can add some grated emerald (the weight of eight grains of barley), and a little rosewater. All this is pounded together into a lump, a bit of which is put into either a cup of wine or a little sorrel syrup, whichever the patient prefers.

When the patient has sweated enough, Katharina puts cloths soaked in herbal extracts over the swellings, again and again. Everyone in the house asks her to stay away from the sick man. She should think of Hänschen and the unborn child. But Katharina is thinking of Jost's mother. A message has been sent to her. She sees the boy's suddenly gaunt face, the dark eyes that keep growing wider and asking their question ever more despairingly. Hänschen has dark eyes like that. And so Katharina battles, full of rage and despair, battles against death. In the kitchen, Aunt Lene keeps busy distilling new juices and potions.

And, lo and behold, the swellings recede. Dr. Schurf is baffled. Word spreads through the whole city: In Luther's house, someone who had the plague has been healed. A miracle! Now Katharina and Aunt Lene are constantly being summoned to other houses.

Word of Jost's recovery even reaches the duke's castle. One morning a wagon pulls up in front of the Black Cloister. A courier shouts from the coach box: "Frau Doktorin should come to the castle. A member of the prince's household has contracted the plague and needs help. Elector Johann requests it!"

Martinus is not home, he is probably at Lufft's printing shop. Aunt Lene is already filling her bag with the medications she will need. She also takes along rubber, euphorbia, and elamite. They are supposed to heighten the effects of the plague egg.

Today Katharina has no eyes for the splendor of the castle, especially since it appears to be empty. All its inhabitants have fled to Torgau, she is told. Only a few of the servants have remained behind, and they are forbidden to leave on pain of punishment. A guard stands outside the gate and lets no one into the castle or out of it unless they have explicit orders.

The maid who brings Katharina and Aunt Lene to a large, elegant bedchamber crosses herself at the door and then immediately disappears. In her eyes is the fear of death. Katharina can just make out a bed with a red canopy. Her heart skips a painful beat when she recognizes the beautiful girl she saw dancing by the Elbe.

"Unfathomable God, how cruel you are." Katharina is so shocked and disconcerted at the sight of the girl, she thinks she sees the grinning figure of death itself standing at the head of the bed. "Lord our God, how can you so cruelly destroy your own work! How can a person who sees such a sight still love you?"

In helpless rage, Katharina washes the pus-filled buboes, some of which have already burst. On the dark splotches that disfigure the girl's white body, she spreads a soothing chamomile ointment. She knows that the miracle she performed on Jost will not be repeated here. Death with its greedy hands has already taken tight hold of this girl. But with the ointment Katharina spreads her compassion, her sudden and overwhelming love for this sweet girl. She sees now that she can't be more than sixteen years old.

"On Saturday she will be seventeen."

Katharina hadn't even noticed that a woman, an elegant woman, is seated at the foot of the bed, almost concealed in the folds of the canopy. She is pressing her folded hands to her mouth. Her face is disfigured by pain and by tears. The fine powder that otherwise serves to brighten her face is now smeared; so is the cinnamon red on her cheeks.

"She is my daughter," the elegant woman says. "And the daughter of Friedrich, the late elector," she adds quietly. Katharina knows that Elector Friedrich had a mistress and children, and now she also knows that she has often seen this woman and her children at church in Torgau. They said the elector had been unable to marry his consort because of class differences.

Aunt Lene begins to administer the hot drink made from the egg to the sick girl, who despite her pain and the nearness of death gazes up at Katharina and Aunt Lene with a thankful and gracious smile. Obediently she gulps it down. Katharina thinks that she is only drinking it for her mother's and for their sake.

Katharina asks the mother the girl's name.

"Benedikta."

Katharina's cloister name. That wasn't necessary for her already profound feelings for the girl to be increased yet further.

"Perform a miracle, God, perform a miracle!"

The girl's eyes follow Katharina as she leaves.

Days later, Katharina learns that Benedikta has died.

✦ ✦ ✦

Now death holds Wittenberg firmly in its clutches. When it comes for Lisbeth, the maid in the Black Cloister, all of Aunt Lene's plague eggs and potions—and all of Katharina's care at the expense of her own health—are of no use. The buboes grow larger and larger, then burst with pus; they cover her whole body, as they did Benedikta's. Along with the maid, two scholars, a scribe, and a law clerk fall ill.

Luther takes charge of caring for these cases. Following Aunt Lene's instructions, he too washes and feeds the patients, wears the same clothes day and night. He doesn't fear the illness himself. Yet when the scholars and the law clerk die, he is despairing and tired. Still, he does not give up. More and more of the sick are brought to the Black Cloister.

The wretched dying continues. The plague bell tolls constantly. Looming like a cloud over the days (which never seem to brighten) is the stench of the disease. The dead stopped receiving proper burial long ago. They are hurriedly left in front of the church, where the plague carts pick them up and dump the bodies into large trenches that have been dug next to the cemetery.

When Hänschen develops a fever and chills, Dr. Schurf and his wife move to the Black Cloister. He fears the worst for the whole family. Martinus and Katharina sit by their little one, who is bright red with fever, but still makes the effort to smile up at his parents. Over and over, Katharina feels up and down his little body, again and again she looks to see whether the fatal splotches have appeared. But after two days the fever disappears like an apparition. Hänschen is weak but healthy. For the whole next day, Katharina doesn't let him out of her arms.

In the first plague-free week, on December 10, 1527, Katharina's second child is born. She names her Elisabeth after the mother of John the Baptist.

Word comes from the Bugenhagen house that Walpurga Bugenhagen has also given birth. It's a boy; his name is Johannes.

Katharina, who had an easy labor, ventures out on the fourth day to the Bugenhagens' to visit mother and child. She brings little Elisabeth and big Hänschen with her. Walpurga is in bed. She is still weak from the birth.

Katharina embraces her friend, whose rather disorderly beauty is reflected in the entire home. Walpurga is a large, ample woman with black curls that poke rebelliously out of her bonnet. And she doesn't care if her corset isn't exactly in place or if her skirt is dusty. Nevertheless, in everything she does she is impressive. Everyone loves her. And so everyone has gathered in the room where she lies: her children, Michael and Sara, the dog, even the maid with the distaff. And here comes Katharina Jonas with her children, Justus and Sophie. Katharina is concerned that things are getting too loud for her friend.

"Oh, no," says Walpurga, and extends her arms to greet Katharina. "How happy I am that we can all be together again."

The Bugenhagens and the Jonases left Wittenberg during the plague. Along with them went many professors and burghers who could afford to seek lodgings elsewhere. In the meantime, most of them have returned. Walpurga got back just in time for the birth, which actually wasn't due for another ten days.

The two newborns are marveled at and compared with each other. Elisabeth, Katharina's daughter, already has a lot of dark hair, but she is quite delicate. Johannes is stockier, and his head is covered with thin, light fuzz.

Katharina is glad to have found good friends in Walpurga Bugenhagen and Katharina Jonas. They are her age and they have both accepted her, the runaway nun, without the slightest reservation. It does Katharina good that the beautiful Walpurga admires her, Katharina's, beauty. And that Katharina Jonas asks her advice when she is getting a new gown. Is that also why she so enjoys visiting in the Cranach house? The master and Barbara often say to her that she is beautiful. Katharina sometimes asks herself whether she is arrogant, as many assert. She doesn't know the answer. She only knows that her friendships signify a little bit of home for her.

Slowly, Katharina walks with her children back across the market square and down to the Black Cloister. In the five years that she has been living in Wittenberg, the city has become familiar to her. Once, after going with Luther to Leipzig and riding back across the new wooden bridge over the Elbe, she is struck with how—when you get right down to it—Wittenberg looks small, dusty gray, and ugly. Though construction is going on everywhere, most of the houses are shacks, most of the people poor and in rags. Yet

Katharina, who until now never felt at home anywhere, does feel at home here. With the good as well as the bad.

✦ ✦ ✦

Little Elisabeth, a gentle child who seldom cries aloud, gets prettier every day. Her eyes are striking. She looks at her mother so knowingly that it touches Katharina deeply. There is something special between her and Elisabeth, something that was not there with Hänschen. When Katharina holds her little daughter in her arms, there is so much sweetness in her heart that it almost hurts.

Martinus asks everyone who sees the little one if they don't find she looks like Katharina. They all say yes, she does. Katharina thinks they're saying so to please Martinus. Privately, she thinks her little daughter doesn't resemble anyone in the family.

"Oh yes she does"—Aunt Lene finally speaks up—"yes she does, Katharina; she looks like your mother."

From that day on, the bond between Katharina and little Elisabeth grows even stronger.

✦ ✦ ✦

Again it is the peak of summer and so hot that everything in the fields and gardens is withering. Many wells are running dry. The two brooks running through the ciy and into the Elbe are murky trickles that stink and daily threaten to dry up entirely. Only the well in the cloister yard, which Katharina had dug very deep, still has plenty of water. Every day, people from the city come to draw water there. Katharina's garden, too, is full and abundant. Once, when

Martinus proudly reports this to his friend Spalatin, Katharina happens to read the letter.

"You see? And you once scolded me on account of that well."

Martinus says that from now on he will always do everything that Katharina orders. Especially when guests are present, he refers to her exclusively as "my lord Käthe."

Hänschen has already picked it up: "Lord Käthe."

Katharina is worried about little Elisabeth. Yesterday, she didn't want to eat her porridge. The child hasn't been sick before, so at first Katharina attributed her lack of appetite to the hot weather. But Elisabeth doesn't want to eat today, either. Aunt Lene gives her honey water to drink, and she takes it thirstily, but she spits it back up. All the while, she remains friendly, looks at her mother with those loving eyes. Katharina rubs the child's tummy with a salve that Aunt Lene has made of rose and quince oils, mixed with wax and the juice of mint greens. Again and again she strokes the little belly. They try to give Elisabeth juices that she will be able to keep down. Blueberry juice with boiled water, rose and quince juices also mixed with water. The little one takes the juice greedily, but soon she spits it all back up.

Now Katharina is overcome with a nameless fear. She calls Dr. Schurf, who just shakes his head about her worry and says that they have done everything right for the child. Elisabeth will surely be back to normal by tomorrow.

Katharina doesn't believe him. Nor does she believe Martinus, who says that Hänschen was sicker than this, and he recovered.

Despite an explicit *no* from Martinus, despite the uncomprehending faces of Aunt Lene and Dr. Schurf, Katharina sends for old Gumppin, who is secretly decried as a witch but is also reputed to have often healed mortally ill children.

Martinus is more than angry. Katharina, who is sitting at her daughter's bedside, hears him declaiming loudly at table. She knows that his words are meant primarily for her ears. "They presume to make children healthy with all sorts of superstition. I wish the children were able to understand and to speak, so they might rebuke their mothers for this great folly. For there is no doubt: They would oppose their mothers and show that they are the wiser ones . . ."

Filled with rage and despair, Katharina finally comes rushing into the main room. There they all sit around the table: Cordatus, Veit Dietrich, Schlaginhaufen, Lauterbach, Weller. All are students of Luther's, and all have eventually become guests at the Black Cloister. They sit there day after day, along with the children and the other house-guests. Recently they have acquired the habit of writing down everything Martinus says at table. Today, Melanchthon is dining there as well. He sees Katharina first and signals to Martinus by nodding in the direction of the door, where she stands trembling. She shouts: "Must I not do everything to save my child?"

Martinus strains to remain calm. "But not in such a way that you carry out the will of the Devil. Either seek natural treatment or call upon God. Would you take this child that God created and offer her up to the wicked enemy?"

"You can only talk like that because you didn't give

birth to her!" Katharina shrieks. "If it would save my Elslein, I'd bring every witch and the Devil himself to her bedside."

All eyes are fixed on Katharina. The maid who is serving the meal crosses herself. Luther sits in stony silence. Melanchthon finally gets up quietly, takes Katharina by the shoulders, and accompanies her back to the child's bed.

In the night, Elisabeth dies.

Two days later, little Johannes Bugenhagen dies also. Comprehending nothing, and devoid of solace, the two mothers embrace.

7

To my amicable, beloved Lord Katharina Lutherin, Doktorin, preacher at Wittenberg.

Dear Lord Käthe! Know that our friendly talks in Marburg are at an end. We are agreed in all things, excepting that the other party holds firmly that there is mere bread in the Eucharist and that Christ is present only in spirit... I think God has blinded them, they have nothing substantial to bring forward...

Kiss Lenchen and Hänschen for me,
your willing servant,
Martinus Luther

✦   ✦   ✦

"Your willing servant. My Lord Käthe." This is how Martinus tries to stay a step ahead of all the gossip concerning his position as husband and master of the house.

After the death of Elisabeth, Katharina was long unable to obey or to pray. Or to sing, either. Not even at Christmas, when Martinus's song of the herald angels rang out in the church: *Vom Himmel hoch da komm ich her.* Not even then was she able to join the singing.

Again and again Katharina goes to the cemetery, to Elisabeth's grave. The little gravestone reads:

Here sleeps Elisabeth,
Martin Luther's little daughter
In the year 1528, August 3

Luther's little daughter. Nobody, nobody in this world, knows how very much she was Katharina's little daughter. Sometimes Katharina would like to just shout it out. She is alone with her sorrow. In the house everyone stays out of her way. For the first time since she escaped the cloister, she has longed to be back at Marienthron. Bound up in Matins, Prime, Terce, Sext, None, Vespers, and Compline, she could let the day glide past without thinking, without acting, without planning. And without praying. She used to fall asleep in the choir; now, she longs for the never-changing, steady rhythm of the liturgy.

Katharina can't even pray to the Mother of God anymore. She just can't. The words of the Psalms do pass her lips, but they're hollow. Katharina's soul is not in it. It seems to her sometimes as if her soul were lying in Elisabeth's little grave. Often she thinks of Benedikta. Is her child's death her punishment for growing angry with God and summoning the witch into her house?

At night, she lies beside Martinus. She is even more alone now than she was as a child in the cloister. She senses that Martinus isn't sleeping either. But he does not turn over toward her. Never have they spoken of the day the child died. Yet it is always there, standing between them.

When Martinus finally does embrace Katharina again, everything within her remains silent.

✦　✦　✦

Coburg Fortress, August 15, 1530
To be delivered into the hands of my dear lord,
Frau Katharin Lutherin in Wittenberg.
My dear Käthe. In these letters from Augsburg you
will see how things stand for our cause in Augsburg.
May God continue to help what he in his grace
began. I cannot write more now, because the courier
is sitting here all ready to go and won't wait any
longer. Give my greetings to Hans and Aunt Lene and
the rest. We are eating ripe grapes now, although it has
been very wet out here.

From my solitude on Assumption Sunday,
Mart. Luther

To the hands of my heartily beloved wife
Katherin Lutherin of Wittenberg.
. . . but I hope we shall be coming ourselves, and that
there soon may be an end to the imperial diet. We
have done enough and made offers, the papists won't
yield a hair's breadth . . .

I have a pretty little book made of sugar for Hans
Luther.

From my solitude on September 8, 1530

. . . they simply want to have the monks and nuns
back in the cloisters. But the elector's chamberlain has

written that he hopes they will leave Augsburg with peace in every alleyway. This seems to be what we all need, because the Turk is preparing to strike at us...

From my solitude on September 10, 1530

✦   ✦   ✦

Katharina is very sad that Martinus never mentions in his letters anything about the death of his father. As much as the loss of the elder Luther hurts Katharina, the thought is more painful to her that Luther is dealing with this sorrow by himself. They are so far apart, Martinus and she. Not only the distance to Coburg separates them. Martinus turns with his doubts, fears, insults, and pain to God. And sometimes to the Devil. But never to his wife. And so he sits in Coburg Fortress, because as an outlaw he is not allowed to leave his land, Saxony. He must stay at Coburg while the imperial diet is held in Augsburg.

And now he writes from Coburg Fortress: "From my solitude..." What sort of solitude does he mean? With his Reformation threatened again and again, does he feel abandoned by God and therefore alone? Or does he miss Melanchthon, who is in Augsburg setting forth the new confession? Or does he long for Hänschen and his young daughter, Magdalena?

Katharina picks up the little girl, who is now a year and a quarter old, from her bed. Magdalena is a May baby. Her birth was quick and not terribly painful. There was no time to fetch the midwife. It was Aunt Lene who received the baby. That is why Magdalena is named after her.

✦   ✦   ✦

The maid comes in and announces that there is a woman at the door and she is asking to speak with Frau Doktorin. Katharina has her invite the woman into the main room.

When Katharina enters the room, Magdalenchen in her arms, she sees a stranger in dusty traveling clothes who is scarcely able to stand. She is very pregnant. Sweat dots her forehead, her lips are cracked, her hair evidently hasn't been combed in days.

"In the name of Christ, help me."

Katharina leads the stranger to a seat by the window. She calls the maid to draw the woman a bath. And here comes Aunt Lene, who has just recovered from a bout of malaria and is still very weak. But she quickly brings the woman a refreshing summer's drink: whey with cinnamon, nutmeg, and violet sugar. The stranger drinks it in one draft, closes her eyes, and leans back against the wall.

"What she needs is a midwife," Aunt Lene announces gruffly, and she sends the maid off to fetch one.

Katharina leads the woman, who introduces herself as Lorichia von Dalberg, to the bath. She gives her a linen smock and instructs the maid to take the woman's dirty but doubtless expensive clothes and wash them. Around her neck Lorichia wears a fine chain with a large ruby surrounded in a handsome setting by many smaller emeralds. Lorichia follows Katharina's eyes and says that it is her last remaining piece of jewelry. Everything else she had to sell during her flight.

Flight? From what?

Lorichia is unable or unwilling to say. And there's no more time for that anyway. Before the maid returns with the midwife, the child is born. Katharina, assisting for the first time, watches, fascinated, as the wreath of hair below Lorichia's abdomen parts, and sure enough, she can see little curls of wet hair in the opening. And now here comes the whole head. Katharina and the maid hold Lorichia's arms while, with infinite care, Aunt Lene twists the little head and shoulders free.

While the maid rubs Lorichia down, first with an herbal solution and then with warm towels, Katharina is filled with delight as she bathes the newborn. Hänschen appears in the doorway, more dragging his wailing sister Magdalena than carrying her. A beaming Katharina shows him the screaming baby boy. She dresses him and lays him in the cradle her children slept in. To give him to his mother would be too dangerous, on account of the evil postnatal flow. Besides, she might roll over and crush the baby in her sleep.

Under the care of Katharina's ointments, oils, and combs, Lorichia grows more beautiful each day. She has a graceful way of tying up her hair so that it surrounds her delicate face like a frame. The more she recovers, the more time she devotes to her appearance. Katharina sees this and is unsure whether to admire Lorichia or be angry with her. Graciously, but also quite regally, Lorichia has the servants doing her bidding as if she were the mistress of the house. And she is puzzled to see Katharina work so much. "Why don't you have more servants?" she asks once. Since there appears to be genuine astonishment (and no malice) behind the question, Katharina cannot reproach her for it.

After all, Lorichia couldn't know that the Luther household is in debt once again.

Just the new house, now being built behind the cloister next to the little garden, costs four hundred gulden. And another one hundred fifty gulden for the roof. This house absolutely has to be finished before winter; otherwise the Black Cloister will not be able to hold the scholars and houseguests that come to Wittenberg from all parts of Germany and consider it the greatest of honors to live in the home of Dr. Luther.

The most famous lodgings in Wittenberg. And the cheapest, Katharina often thinks irritably. She still hasn't been permitted to raise the room and board fee she charges the scholars, some of whom come from wealthy homes. Katharina still doesn't know where she will get the one hundred thirty gulden she needs for the brewery. And she was so happy when Elector Johann granted her brewing privileges.

Money, money, money. How would Katharina feed and clothe more servants? It's easy for Lorichia to talk. She is obviously from a wealthy home. But she never speaks about it. Nor does Katharina ask.

Martinus, who returns from Coburg Fortress at the end of October, wants to know from Katharina, immediately, where Lorichia comes from and why. When Katharina tells him that Lorichia isn't saying, he asks her himself in his direct way. And Katharina watches in amazement as Lorichia replies with exquisitely courteous, gracious, and occasionally despairing words and gestures, until Martinus asks no more questions. He doesn't even appear put off at her continued refusal to reveal even a little about herself.

Soon Lorichia is the central figure at the Luther table. She does say that she is originally from the city of Cologne on the Rhine. And that she is astonished to find burghers' wives in Wittenberg evidently so little engaged in commercial ventures. In Cologne, many women are organized into guilds of gold spinners, for example, or silk makers, or yarn makers. Some of them work together with their husbands, who are engaged in the import and export trade as silk traders and town councillors, and thus acquire great wealth. "The women of Cologne," says Lorichia, "but also some in Frankfurt and Nuremberg, deal in spices, in metal and steel."

As fascinated as Katharina is with what Lorichia has to tell, she is displeased that Martinus is engaging her more and more often in conversation. At table, he passes her the saltcellar, the bread. He even refills her wine glass.

Has he ever been that attentive to Katharina?

In these days Katharina lives up to her reputation as a quick-tongued, overbearing domina whose word is law in the Luther household. She sweeps through the house with skirts flying, snarls at the maid when she fails to return on time from the market, scolds Wolf, saying she'll have to order him a set of tools that move by themselves, since he keeps falling asleep over his work.

When she sees the smoked pork and the vegetables she labored to gather from every corner of the garden, this meal she prepared with such care, getting cold while everyone goes on talking and disputing, she slams down her wine goblet: "Why do you talk endlessly and not eat? Do you think I spend my mornings in the kitchen for you just for fun?"

And to Cordatus, who keeps his writing things next to his plate so he can take down everything he hears, she says, "So, Cordatus, you can write all that down, too. You keep writing things that are nobody's business anyway."

As always when Katharina speaks her mind all too forcefully, she feels uncomfortable afterward. It isn't just the table guests that provoke her anger. (Although she does not like having them trumpet out every word that is spoken, and then slant things unfairly. Do they really think she, Katharina, won't find out what they write?)

No, it isn't the table guests. It's really Lorichia who makes Katharina furious, though it's actually not her fault. Just now she is grinding coal into the finest powder so she can use a fine brush to trace a line just above her eyelashes. That looks beautiful against her light hair. (Suddenly, Katharina recalls that Benedikta's eyes, too, were darkened this way.) Lorichia also mixes the finest flour with a little earth, presses it through a linen cloth, and uses it to powder her forehead and nose. She does this so skillfully that no one who didn't see her do it notices a thing. And the men least of all. They all admire Lorichia. Even Melanchthon casts a shy glance her way. So does Martinus. His eyes follow Lorichia when she leaves the room. Isn't he secretly looking at her at table as well? And when is the last time he embraced her, Katharina?

Katharina forgets entirely that lately she hasn't wanted him to. Privately, she was quite happy that Martinus was away from home. If she got lonely at night, she would bring Hänschen and Lenchen into her bed.

Katharina convinces herself that Martinus only has eyes for Lorichia. And Lorichia hangs with admiring eyes on his every word. She is always asking him how things stand for the Protestant cause. And where he gets the strength to take on the papists day after day. Martinus's reply is confident and cheerful, as he seldom enough really is: "If Christ is not with us, I ask you, where is he present in the world? If *we* are not the church or a part of the church, where is the church? If *we* do not have the Word of God, who does have it? If *we* fall, Christ falls with us, and he is the ruler of the world. And even if he does fall—I'd rather fall with Christ than stand with the emperor!"

Yes, Lorichia cultivates the right conversational tone with Martinus, Katharina understands that very well. Lorichia shows him all the respect and esteem that is due the famous reformer. By contrast, the burning question on Katharina's mind is how to protect her expensive mother sows from this last outbreak of the swine plague, which has already claimed four of her pigs.

Still, no matter how inadequate she, Katharina, may be, Martinus is her wedded husband. And though he may be less than attentive, he belongs to her, to Katharina. And the Devil can come over her with all his demons before she will concede even one of Martinus's thoughts to Lorichia.

✦　✦　✦

Katharina decides first of all to take a bath and wash her hair. She has discovered that she can do her best thinking at bath time.

The two maids have already set the table for supper. Today there are only flatbreads, cheese, and fruit from the Luthers' garden. Apples, pears, nuts, cucumbers. The black chest is empty again. Katharina has just finished with her toilette, apart from her hair's being not quite dry. In any case, she smells of the fragrant almond oil she rubbed into her skin after her bath, and her eyes are lined with black like Lorichia's. She even is wearing the powder on her forehead and nose. And of all people, it is Lorichia who says, as if seeing Katharina for the first time, "You look beautiful, Katharina Lutherin."

All eyes are on Katharina, so much so that she grows uncomfortable. But not too uncomfortable. She tosses her hair back and offers Martinus the pear she has just quartered.

Surprised, he takes the fruit, and their eyes meet. Katharina feels the fire that she thought had gone out now taking hold of her whole body. And she also senses that the same thing is happening to Martinus. Inside Katharina there is a humming and a tingling from her toes up to her head.

Her Soul whispers delightedly: We will put our arms around each other.

Her Head replies: So what? Since your wedding day, you've done that at least five hundred times!

Soul: But today it's different.

Head: Different? How?

Soul: Today I want it, today I'm happy, today I have a longing for it.

Head: I guess you've completely forgotten what Paul

says in Romans 7: "With my flesh I serve the law of sin!" You know, after all, that God is lenient with married couples only because their lying together can be blessed with children.

Soul: God. I'm always hearing only about God. Didn't he make human beings? Thus he also made me, the soul. Why did he make it that I always get so excited when we hold each other?

Head: I ask myself the same question, especially when you scream and moan so loudly. Sometimes it's downright embarrassing.

Soul: Don't you understand that I'm so loud only because I know God forbids it?

Head: No, I don't understand that.

Soul: I don't quite understand it myself, so how could you get it into all your complex branchings? Once again: I suddenly felt hot. And then I knew that I wanted to tenderly embrace Martinus for who he is. For his eyes that grow deep then and fiery. For his skin that gleams like gold then and is a little moist. For all his limbs that do me a world of good in their embrace. That make me fly up, high above our bed, above the Black Cloister, above Wittenberg, and off into fiery golden spaces that I do not know and cannot name. Into spaces that, once you've been there, you want to return to again and again.

Head: I want to say something.

Soul: No. I'm in charge tonight. Tomorrow morning I'll have urgent need of you again. You'll have to dictate a letter for me to Chancellor Brück, that slanderous ducat counter. Until then you restrain yourself. Too often, you block my view. You are very thick and very hard, head. That's not your doing, I know, but you make it hard for me. Because of you, I often can't really see Martinus. You always want to be right. When Martinus wrote in three letters "from solitude," you immediately said that he was talking about Melanchthon and about Hänsichen and Lenichen. You never gave me a chance to read it myself. When will you finally stop dominating me?

8

CONSTRUCTION IS GOING ON around the Black Cloister. But this time, Katharina is not the one responsible for it. The Turks under their sultan, Suleiman, have advanced far into Hungary, and they are becoming more and more of a threat. Therefore the elector is having his capital, Wittenberg, fortified. The walls of the city are being reinforced and raised, especially the protruding corners, which are most exposed to a frontal assault. The southeast corner, where the Black Cloister meets the city wall, is to be shielded by a mighty bastion surrounding the rear house and the cloister garden in a semicircle. Although the elector gave the command that the construction work not come too close to Luther, the master of ordnance, Friedrich von der Grune, still has the whole courtyard filled level with the house's upper floor.

This has Martinus furious. He demands that the fill be carted away. When this does not happen, he shouts at von der Grune: "Of one thing you can be sure—I will not yield one hair's breadth further to the accursed construction with which you are clearing out the contents of my lord's purse."

Martinus wants all damage done to the brewery door

repaired; he wants guarantees that the garden wall and the new house will not be harmed. He never tires of cursing the elector's master of ordnance: "That man is God's and my enemy," he says to Katharina.

Katharina is glad that Martinus is paying attention to the property at all. There is more and more of it. They have purchased a garden by the oak-tree marsh and a large orch-ard behind the swine market. One advantage of the latter is that a lazy brook flows through it, forming a little pond. They have already been fishing there. Now Katharina can put pike, loach, trout, perch, and carp on the table.

The cellar, which was finished last summer, is lined with earthenware pots of cherries, pears, apples, and peaches that Katharina and the maids harvested and preserved.

All this is absolutely essential. Katharina and Martin now have thirteen children—nine adopted children and four of their own. Hans and Magdalena Luther have been joined by two brothers. Martinchen turned two on November 9, and Paul is now four months old. On January 28, he came into the world and was baptized at the elector's castle the same night. At the dinner that followed, Martinus said that he could readily have had all three of his sons baptized under the name Paul—so indebted is he to the Apostle Paul.

The godparents of the youngest son are Duke Johann Ernst of Saxony; the elector's ancestral marshal, Hans Löser; Justus Jonas; Melanchthon; and the wife of the elec-tor's personal physician, Kaspar Lindemann.

✦ ✦ ✦

A few days after the birth, Katharina writes to Ave:

Grace and peace, dearest Ave.

In Marienthron they are at Compline now, and here I sit at the table of my Martinus. Only here do I have some measure of quiet to finally write you this letter. I know that you understand and forgive my negligence; you have a large household and a famous husband yourself. I hear that awful illness, the English sweat, has broken out again in your area, so I suppose you don't get to see your husband very often, either. Martinus is in Wittenberg, but not here with me just now. He has gone with Melanchthon, Jonas, and Bugenhagen to see Lucas Cranach. He is beginning a large altarpiece for our church. It is to have three panels, with Baptism and Last Supper, and Lucas wants to include portraits of all the reformers.

Barbara gave me a kiss to pass along to you. God be praised, her attacks of melancholia aren't so severe anymore. But sometimes I still really have my hands full with her . . . No, dearest Ave, don't be worried. You know how quick I am with my words. At least that's what Martinus often says. He said so yesterday. We have an Englishman staying with us, his name is Robert Varnes, and they chased him out of England because he has become a Protestant. This greatly learned man does not understand the German language. Martinus said to him: "I give you my wife to be your preceptor. She will teach you the German language. For she has a ready tongue and knows it so thoroughly that she far outdoes me in that regard."

And then, dear Ave, he turned right around and made me furious again. For he added: "True, when women have a ready tongue it is not always a thing to be praised. It suits them better to stammer and not be able to speak well. That becomes them much better."

Can you understand, dearest Ave, that I could have thrown the soup pot at him right then and there? Maybe you think to yourself that I am possessed by the Devil (from our years at the cloister you would have good reason to do so), but believe me, Ave, this Black Cloister where I've lived for eight years now and made the beds for more and more people, this Black Cloister is a boardinghouse, a hospital, and a madhouse (sometimes more hospital, sometimes more madhouse, but mostly all three together). If I didn't remind each one of his place and his duties, Ave, things would get even more confused and chaotic than they are now. Can you imagine that I simply couldn't afford to stammer?

If they weren't afraid of me, Ave, they would cheat and lie to my Martinus even more, and pluck him like the goose on St. Martin's Day. But he simply refuses to see it!

Ave, isn't this whole business of being married rather strange? (You're the only one I can talk to about it, my letters don't get trumpeted around the world like those of Martinus.) It has gotten so that I don't understand myself anymore. Sometimes during our nights I am so at one with Martinus that I can't imagine ever speaking a harsh word to him. And then you should see me sometimes during the day!

It's the same with the children. Did you know, Ave, that we have thirteen now? From Sister Kaufmann alone we have the six orphans. Andreas and Cyriakus are Hänschen's age. Fabian, Georg, Elschen, and Lenchen are (in that order) each a year younger. Then there are our own four children—you still haven't seen the two youngest ones, Martinchen and Paul. Martinchen is full of mischief, and Paulus does not like me to dress him. He fights me off with both hands and feet, so much so that this morning Martinus commented that he should go right ahead and defend himself, like his father who always had to fight to keep the Pope from tying him down.

With so many children it often seems like the Devil is in charge; you don't need to hear any details to imagine what it's like. One always has the measles, chicken pox, malaria, or the croup that nearly took away Fabian last week. One is always teething; right now it's Elschen. One has always bumped into something, or the others did it to him. They hit, choke, and bite each other; sometimes it gets so bad I can't bear to watch. But then they'll all be playing together again, and they're a joy to be around. Especially my Hänsichen. And Lenichen, my Magdalena! She is four now, and she loves her brother so completely—I've never seen the like between siblings. And Hänsichen would go through the fires of Purgatory for her, too.

Although I thank God that we have healthy children, I am often so hard on them. That worries me profoundly, and I can't tell anyone about it, only you, because I know that you love me. But I wonder if you can see through my fingers that far too often I punish even the very little ones? Sometimes, when the Devil really has me in his claws, the children seem like a pack of hunting dogs, all chasing after me. And at that moment I am so afraid of them—and that's why I kick and I hit and I scream and yell.

Ach, Ave, the worst of it is that I don't love the orphaned children the way I love my own. Still, it's strange—I'm far more patient with the adopted children than with my own flesh and blood.

Do you understand, Ave, why we're always hardest on the ones we love most?

Dearest Ave, today is the ninth of May already, and still my letter lies here, unfinished. I started it last Saturday, and now it's come round Friday again already. The house is finally quiet. From time to time I do have to jump up and see after Martinchen; he has an earache that started yesterday, and he's been crying a lot. I heated him up a bag of chamomile and stone clover and put it on his ear. He doesn't pull it off, because he can feel that it's helping. Martinus is still awake. He's writing a church order for Brandenburg-Ansbach and Nuremberg. If only the rest of the world had some order to it as well. But intrigues are everywhere. So it's no use having imperial diets and the Augsburg Confession and the Schmalkaldic League.

Nor do they tire of singing satirical songs about us. They depict Martinus as a fat sack who has to carry his belly around on a wheelbarrow. (Actually he's not fat at all, just a little more stately and robust than he used to be.) On his back he carries a basket containing all the reformers and his writings. They show me wearing a habit, trudging along behind with a baby and a dog.

Two magisters from Leipzig, von der Heyden and Hasenberg are their names, clang the swine bell especially harshly against us. In one drama, they have Martinus burned at the stake, and for me they invent affairs with students.

Ach, Ave, even if we go on living for many more years or go far away—say, to that new land, America—we'll never completely put the cloister behind us.

But I've been a target for ten years now, and it doesn't bother me much.

Though there was one particularly nasty attack recently. The elector's chancellor, Brück, do you recall the name? I wish him plague, cholera, and pox. He has two cloven hooves, and he has been spewing from that foul-smelling maw of his something to the effect that I had been stealing money from our old Wolf Sieberger! Did you ever meet my dear, sweet Wolf? In case you haven't, I'll have to start by telling you about him.

Martinus and Father Staupitz journeyed to the duchy of Bavaria in the spring of 1517, and they came to the city of Munich. Martinus preached there in the Augustinian church. But Munich is a thoroughly papist city, and later on they drowned three women in a river named Isar and beheaded six men on account of their Protestant beliefs. So Wolf Sieberger fled Munich and came to Wittenberg—and to Martinus, eventually becoming his famulus.

And then, as you know, I came and took charge of the Black Cloister. He had a hard time getting used to me, did my Wolf, but we've grown fond of each other since. One thing is true: you simply cannot watch him work. Just recently, Martinus wrote to Link in Nuremberg requesting tools for Wolf that, if possible, would move by themselves. And there you have it in a nutshell: my Wolf likes to dream. And sometimes I ask myself if he hasn't got the right idea. We have all seen how many troubles and tears come from too active a mind, from high scholarly endeavors, and from restless creative energy.

I'd rather listen to my Wolf. He speaks more and more often of Munich. I enjoy his speech, it's full of As and Rs, and he rumbles and rolls his Rs so softly.

And they say I stole from him? Wolf has always taken his pay from the elector, just as Martinus does, and put it into the black chest. He still does—and without a word from me or Martinus. And now they're saying that I with my extravagant ways am taking everything from him. Wolf himself just says:

"Let 'em say what they will." (Bavarians don't like to talk much.)

But it makes my bile boil, I'm so angry . . .

Dearest Ave, I hear that the courier won't be by again until Tuesday. So I'll have a chance to tell you about Lorichia, you'll remember I spoke of her in my last letter. As you know, she always kept a mantle of silence over her affairs.

Well, we're sitting at table one morning, Hänsichen has just said the blessing, and there's a knock at the door. No sooner does the maid announce one Hartmut von Cronberg, than Lorichia leaps up from the table as if possessed by the Devil and races to her room. I'd never seen her gather up her skirts so quickly!

And then we found out the truth. Lorichia was married in Worms (a city on the Rhine) to the nobleman Wolf von Dalberg. It happened that he died, and as a young widow she was secretly married and then spirited off by a wealthy Jew named Jakob, whom she loved very much. Not until they reached Erfurt did her relatives find even a trace of her. There they hired horsemen who were to pursue the couple and bring her back. By chance, they encountered the Jew, Jakob, on the street, riding along on his high horse like a nobleman. They cut him down. Lorichia continued her flight by herself—and the rest you know. She wasn't always kind to me, but seeing her fear I would rather have kept her here than hand her over to that proud brother of hers. Praise God, Martinus did succeed in reconciling the two of them . . .

Dearest Ave, the day was long and bright, but now the night claims its due. More than once, my Martinus has given me greetings to relay to you; as I'm sure you know, he is still fond of you.

May God be with you. Monday, June 13, 1533
Katharina Lutherin

9

A COLD FEBRUARY DAY in the year 1537

Snow and chunks of ice cover the road between Schmalk-alden and Tambach. Two coaches bearing the elector of Saxony's coat of arms bump and jostle along. Semmel-hans, the son of a peasant, holds the reins on the first one. He curses, "Let the Devil come swinging his pitchfork and flail. Here we are driving a nice, warm fire around, but we get to freeze our asses off."

The first wagon is followed by a smaller one, containing two copper pans in which glowing coals are constantly being tended.

A postal courier overtakes them. He calls to the coach-man that he has an urgent letter to take to Luther's wife in Wittenberg. "I'm supposed to make it to Wittenberg by tomorrow," shouts the courier.

"I hope his horse breaks a leg before he gets there." The coachman cracks his whip: "I could be warm right now at Wilhelmsburg in Schmalkalden, but no, I have to drive Dr. Bigmouth around. Some character he is, learns Latin and Greek and Jewish and who knows what else, and then he promises us truth and justice! But then as soon as his patron, the elector, dies, he hands the likes of us over to the sword. *Against the Thieving and Murdering Hordes of Peasants.* Written by that fellow back there! I've got half a mind to toss those pans into the snow. Then the fellow behind me would have a cold ass, too. Hya! Hya, you sorry horses— the Devil ride you straight to Hell!"

The horses pull and the coach suddenly speeds up, tossing the sick man inside around violently. He shouts—and all at once, his bladder empties for the first time in days. He sighs with relief. Half asleep, he whispers: "Katharina, my dearest, not a drop has come out of me for so long, I wasn't sleeping, couldn't keep food down or drink. Summa: I've been dead. I had commended you and the children to God, especially little Maruschel. But now the tears of many people have been powerful enough that on the road here God has opened the passage of my bladder and surely a small room full of water has passed from me. I feel like a man reborn.

"Katharina, my prince has sent riders so that you might come to meet my coach in case I might die. That is no longer necessary, and you can stay at home. You know how glad I would be to hold you in my arms, if I could . . ."

✦   ✦   ✦

Grimma, March 1, 1537
In the White Lamb Inn, Katharina, with little Maruschel on her lap, and Lucas Cranach are sitting on the bench by a window. They are waiting for the coach that is to bring Luther. Cranach takes a long drink from his beer stein and then holds out both arms toward the child. "Give me Maruschel for a while, Katharina, your arms must be numb

by now. Besides, I need to get into practice; I hope my son Johannes will be returning soon from Italy and bringing Agneta Hohnfelder with him. Barbara and I are waiting for grandchildren."

Cranach swings Maruschel back and forth, and the little girl repays him with happy squeals and gurgles.

Maruschel is already a good two years old, thinks Katharina. When she came into this world, on December 17, 1534, it was just such a jarringly cold day. Little Margarete's godfather, Prince Joachim von Anhalt, didn't come to the baptism because of the harsh weather, but he sent the court preacher, Nikolaus Hausmann (who brought a truly princely gift), in his place. The second godfather is Dr. Jakob Propst, once a friar with Luther in Wittenberg and now superintendent in Bremen. Martinus was especially loving in commending Maruschel to him. Katharina sighs: Maruschel has very old parents. How long will we be able to keep on caring for her?

Maruschel has something else on her mind: She's trying to pull off Cranach's biretta. Squealing with delight, she reaches up into his hair. She is evidently very interested in his nostrils. And when he closes his eyes, she tries again and again to pry them open. Katharina has brought Maruschel along on this journey to Grimma because Martinus is particularly attached to his youngest daughter. Maruschel is filled with such a glowing joy of living, she can be so impetuously affectionate, that Martinus sometimes be-comes utterly absorbed in playing with her. Katharina can still hear the sound of his words: "Maruschel is like a drunk. She does not know that she is living. She is completely happy and secure, she hops and she jumps. Such children like to be in large, open rooms where they have plenty of space."

Space. Again, Katharina heaves an involuntary sigh. She can't add on to the Black Cloister fast enough to keep it from getting crowded again. For the past year, Magister Agricola from Eisleben and his wife, Else, and their nine children have been living in the Black Cloister. When they came to Wittenberg, there was an outbreak of cholera, and the Black Cloister was the only house that was spared. So Luther suggested that Agricola, who had found no quarters in the disease-ravaged city, move into the Black Cloister. And they have stayed. Katharina has not regretted having them. Else Agricola is gentle and yet thoroughly practical and quite energetic. Katharina is glad she can rely on her. Just now, for example, when she can ride out to meet Martinus, knowing that she can leave Else in charge at the Black Cloister . . . The innkeeper enters the room and announces to his guests that the elector's coaches have arrived.

Katharina rushes out; Cranach follows with Maruschel. Katharina sees the coachman slapping his body with his arms, again and again. He is frozen red and blue, and now he is trying in vain to free the icy bridles from the horses' heads. Katharina quickly walks up to the coachman and hands him the rest of her travel money.

With mouth agape, the coachman watches her gently help his hated passenger down from the wagon and hold up a little child for a kiss. Now the coachman feels the cold more than ever. Furiously, he slaps his arms against his body. Again and again.

Martinus feels weak, but he has no more pain. The copper pans from the elector's coach can be loaded onto Cranach's wagon along with Luther's bedding. Martinus wants to head right home to Wittenberg. Katharina is glad of it. She misses the children. Magdalena in particular will be happy when her parents are back. She is eight years old now, and she looks like her brother Hans in girls' clothing. Everyone is amazed at the similarity between the two. Magdalena has a delicate face; sometimes Katharina thinks it could be of porcelain, with that high, rounded forehead, those paintbrush-fine pale blond brows that, like Katharina's, seem to flow in one line down into the curve of her nose. Her mouth, too, is like Katharina's—the upper lip narrow, the lower part of her mouth fuller. In all this delicate paleness, Martinus's dark eyes provide a fascinating contrast.

Oh, how Katharina loves to dress her big daughter up! On Sunday mornings, when she helps her into the long, white dress with the high, frilled collar, her pride in this stunningly beautiful child is such that she can scarcely hide it from the others. Katharina knows that Martinus is proud and happy, too. While he was at Coburg Fortress, she sent him a picture of Magdalena. He immediately tacked it up over his writing table and looked at it again and again.

Katharina sees Luther gazing tenderly at the sleeping Maruschel. The little girl's fine hair is flattened in ringlets against her head. Deep sleep makes her round and otherwise cheerful face look serious and infinitely wise. The little mouth—it is Martinus's mouth—is closed. The upper lip displays an unmistakable M, while the lower lip is full and soft.

Katharina catches Martinus's eye. Smiling, she gestures toward Maruschel's mouth and says, "Do you see how her mouth forms an M? M like Maruschel, Margarete, Martinus."

But Martinus is looking at Katharina. Quietly he says, "You are more precious to me than the kingdom of France and the domains of Venice. God gave you to me—and me to you."

Since Katharina doesn't answer, the only sounds are Cranach's occasional snoring, the jostling of the wagon, and the clop-clop of the horses' hooves.

Martinus takes Katharina's hand: "I missed you all terribly yesterday in Schmalkalden, as I lay deathly ill. I thought I would not see you again. How painful my separation from you all was." Katharina presses Martinus's hand and leans forward toward him, for now he is speaking even more quietly, almost more to himself: "I do believe that such natural affection and love, as a man has for his wife and children, are greatest in people about to die."

Now Martinus looks again into Katharina's eyes. He draws her hand onto his breast, and she hears his heart pounding as he says, "It is a great thing, the bond and the shared life between man and wife."

Katharina straightens up. Suddenly she is painfully aware of every muscle in her back. She is cold. She pulls the blanket closer around her.

It is a great thing, the bond . . . Katharina has heard that phrase before. Martinus preached about marriage at the start of the new year. He composed a song just for this sermon:

As man and wife in peace to dwell
To share in joys and trials as well
To be one flesh, one heart and soul
This grace, Lord God, on them bestow.

✦   ✦   ✦

Every time Martinus preaches, the thought crosses Katharina's mind that he is far more strongly wedded to the church than to her, Katharina. Here in church, the people's eyes hang on his lips. Especially when he speaks about marriage.

> The state of matrimony is, next to religion, the highest state on earth. But people, like the cattle in the field and the dregs of the world, flee from it for fear of personal hardship. But by trying to avoid the rain they fall into the water. So come ahead, in the name of the Lord, and each take up his own cross! It is God's order and commandment that we fulfill our duty to produce offspring. And if it weren't for this reason, we should still consider that marriage is a medicine that fights sin because it reduces unchastity . . .

Again and again in the course of the sermon, Martinus's rage flared up against the papists, who have never stopped vilifying the Protestants for marrying. Katharina knows that this thorn in his flesh allows Martinus no peace.

> Many of us poor Lutherans have taken wives, so you

think here's finally something you can find fault with, since there's nothing else you can use to strike and harass us, so as to distract from and conceal all your scandalous, licentious whoring, the rape of all the cloisters complete with your cruelties and unbishop-like vices that disgrace and defile all Christendom. That way—as pure innocents who have never so much as harmed a fly—you can grab all power for yourselves! But proceed with caution, dear sirs! You'll be surprised how masterfully we sweep away your whores and stolen wives. You will have to stand before both God and the world and be named and judged as whoremongers and whorekeepers. We will paint for the world such a picture of your Roman Sodom, your Italian wedding, your Venetian and Turkish brides and your Florentine bridegroom, Pope Clement di Medici, that you will be able to see and feel just how our marriage takes revenge against your unwedded chastity . . .

Then Martinus spoke softly again:

...Those who are not yet in the state of marriage think it is a life of bliss, but those who are in it think quite differently . . .

It seemed to Katharina as if the whole congregation around her were inwardly breathing a collective sigh. Martinus went on,

That is why God tolerates the passion he gave to husband and wife. He thinks, "I have to give the fool a pretty cap. For if it were not so, people would never choose married life." And if passion and love were always present, then one spouse would devour the other out of sheer love, as the proverb has it. And so the Devil is the sworn enemy of the state of marriage, as he is of all God's word and works, making man and wife often resist each other, forget their love, grow impatient, and yet they must remain joined together . . .

Then Martinus closed his sermon with the sentence that it is a great thing, the bond between man and wife.

In the creaking and jostling coach just now crossing the bridge over the Elbe into Wittenberg, Katharina suddenly realizes how tired she is. All her limbs hurt. She would like to sleep. Not to think about the fact that there is nothing that belongs to her. Martinus's words and desires and sufferings don't belong to her. They belong to him, to the church, to the elector. Just as the Black Cloister, where Katharina makes her home, belongs to Martinus and the elector (who recently made the deed over to his Luther). And the children? Do they belong to her, or to Martinus, or to God?

Now the coach pulls into the courtyard, and children come pouring out of the Black Cloister. Then come Else Agricola and Katharina Jonas and Walpurga Bugenhagen.

Why are they all so strangely quiet? Only now does Katharina see Barbara Cranach standing motionless in the doorway. Young Lucas pulls away from her arms and runs sobbing to his father: "Our Johannes, father, he's not coming home ever again. He died in Bologna!"

Katharina rushes to Barbara, clutching her in sudden fear. Our children, who do our children belong to? Barbara is staring with empty eyes. Her voice is dangerously calm as she says over and over, "He was so looking forward to Italy. He wanted to see Michelangelo and Raphael . . . My Johannes, my little Hans . . ."

10

Rothenburg bei Fulda. March 5, 1540

Today Landgrave Philipp von Hessen is secretly marrying Hoffräulein Margarete von Saale. Secretly—because the landgrave is married and has ten children. Still, he cannot part with the hoffräulein, and so he has pleaded with Martinus and Melanchthon to help him. The two advised him for heaven's sake to marry the girl he loves, but to keep everything strictly secret. What an illusion. Like a tidal wave the rumor spills across the land and threatens to poison the fruits of the Reformation. Melanchthon, who was present at the wedding, falls gravely ill with remorse and fury at his mistaken decision, which will eventually become the turning point in the power struggle between the emperor and the Protestants.

Katharina feels tired, just tired. She saw that Martinus and Philippus were impressed with the crisis of conscience the landgrave described to them. And now? Emotions are being exploited for political ends. There is not one impulse in this world that can't be turned into power and money. The holy fury of the peasants, the hunger for God's truth, the passion between a man and a woman. For the powerful, nothing is sacred.

Katharina would really like to leave the Black Cloister

and settle permanently with all the children in Zulsdorf. From his inheritance, Martinus bought her the estate (which until now belonged to the von Bora family and can no longer be kept up by her stepbrothers). This little estate, which consists of only a manor house, a stable, a barn, and three thresher cottages, is a place of refuge for Katharina. When the plague bell rang in Wittenberg again last year, she brought the children and servants to safety there. When Martinus writes her, he calls her Katharina von Bora und Zulsdorf. On account of the garden by the swine market, he calls her Swinemarketwife, Gardener. Another time he writes to her as Preacher, Doktorin, Brewmistress, and all the other things she can be . . .

All the other things she can be. Katharina has been having dreams rather often again (especially on nights when Martinus is away)—dreams that stay with her and occupy her thoughts the following day. She can scarcely sleep, so much do her thoughts revolve around the estate. The pigs, horses, cattle that belong to the Zulsdorf estate, and those at the Black Cloister as well, need fodder and care. In addition, soon she must come up with twenty-four bushels each of grain and oats for planting. But there's no money. Might her neighbor in Zulsdorf lend it to her? The manor house is in urgent need of repair. The roof has begun leaking. Maybe she can fell some trees in the Zulsdorf forest and sell them.

If only she weren't so constantly tired. Katharina is pregnant again. Though it's May already and everything is sprouting and reaching up toward the warm sun, Katharina is always cold. Else Agricola grates red and white coral for her into rosewater that she has sweetened with violet sugar. Every morning she brings porridge to Katharina's room, so she can eat it before she gets out of bed. But it's to no avail: Katharina vomits it all back up, and she keeps vomiting until the bitter bile comes.

I'm too old, Katharina thinks, far too old. In January, she turned forty-one. Other women have long since started holding grandchildren in their arms. Katharina's youngest, Maruschel-Margarete, is now five. Katharina had hoped that she wouldn't be getting pregnant anymore. And now it has happened after all. Everything is different with this pregnancy. In her fourth month now, she's still having the constant vomiting, the abdominal cramps, the stabbing pains in her back.

When she suddenly begins bleeding, Katharina is sure she is going to die. She saw it happen to Else Cruziger and to the weaver's wife. The blood just gushes out; in a few minutes, her bed is soaked. Katharina sees the horror in Martinus's eyes.

He fetches Dr. Schurf, calls Else Agricola, Justus and Katharina Jonas. The Bugenhagens come. So do Lucas and Barbara Cranach. A distraught Melanchthon, recently recovered from a severe illness himself, holds Katharina by the shoulders. His wife stands silently by the door.

Katharina sees all this and, in an almost pleasant way, she is indifferent to it. She also sees her children weeping and praying. Hans pressing his fist to his mouth, Magdalena clinging to him. Little Martin and Paulus sitting in front of the bed and staring openmouthed at their mother. Maruschel sobbing as Martinus holds her. Katharina sees it, and she feels nothing. She is falling deeper and deeper into flaming veils, and all she wants to do is keep falling, falling, falling.

Then she sees Martinus's face again. It's as if his face were made of stone. A stone with two black coals in it. Why did he go and bring the others? Why doesn't he stay here alone with Katharina and with death?

Martinus should go away, they should all go away. Melanchthon, too. Yes, him too. His fingers are still clenched around Katharina's shoulders. She hears his words: "God, leave her here with us."

Oh, no. Katharina doesn't even want to stay with Melanchthon. They should all go away, so she can finally have her dance with death. Until now, she has always hated, cursed, and feared him, the grinning figure with his scythe. But: He's not ugly at all, why, he's Hieronymus! Katharina hears Martinus calling, "Your flame, Amyntas, your old beloved!"

Lovely Hieronymus, you've been captured by Knight Rosenberg, I know, you're in a dark dungeon. Martinus is pleading for you everywhere, but I'm not. Now I can say it, now that I'm dying. I consider it right that you are in chains. That your wife is distressed. How gladly would I weep about it, but I am not a good soul. My soul is full of hatred. I have never forgiven you, and I never will. I won't forgive anybody. Not even on my deathbed. This is the time for truth, sweet Hieronymus. Maybe you're dying in your chains, too, you great, distinguished city councillor of Nuremberg. Then we could have a wedding. My veil would be made of red and gray flames, and our crest would be the scythe, the scythe with the skull. Hieronymus . . . I'm tired. But never too tired to hate . . .

The veils around Katharina tear away, dissolve into foul-smelling vapors.

Katharina is confused. Can this be Hell? Finally, she is completely awake, and in her nostrils there is a nauseating stench. Dr. Schurf has set fire to some partridge feathers and is holding the smoldering bundle under her nose. Else and Barbara bind up Katharina's arms and legs in linen bandages so tightly that she could scream. First they give her pepper to smell, and then smelling apples they have made from wax, citronella, nutmeg, cloves, borage, and ambergris. Katharina knows they will do everything they can to keep her from losing consciousness again. She used this same treatment last summer, when Aunt Lene died. She came down with a high fever that wouldn't break for days, and finally fell into a deep coma. Katharina took turns with Martinus and Dr. Schurf. For days they fought to save her. Death was stronger. Half of Wittenberg mourned with Katharina. Martinus, too. He had loved Aunt Lene very much.

Together with Katharina, he mourned as if for a mother . . .

But Katharina's strong constitution finally overcomes her illness.

11

It is July, and late into the afternoon heat blankets the town, so heavy and damp it feels like walking in an invisible warm fog. Katharina is picking flowers and sprigs in her new garden by the Els woods. Wolf Sieberger is puttering around on a bird trap. He interrupts his work to help her sprinkle the sprigs with water and lay them on a little wagon. On their way home the two of them pass the hops garden, which Katharina has also recently acquired, on the bank of the Specke.

"Good thing you bought that," Wolf says to Katharina. "Hops are getting more expensive every day if you buy from the peasants."

Katharina knows that her Wolf is saying this to make her feel good. He always agrees with everything Katharina does, even before she does it. He goes with her to Zulsdorf, and advises her to lease the Boo property as well. Martinus, who is just now working on his will, asked Wolf whether after his (Luther's) death, he would rather live alone or stay with the family. Wolf said that without his father Martinus Luther he wouldn't like to live at all. But if it had to be, he would definitely rather stay with Katharina and the children.

Wolf understands that Katharina's land purchases and leases are nothing more than a race against old age, which could soon make it impossible for her and Martinus to provide a home for their children. Katharina would like to furnish each child with a mighty fortress. The adopted ones included.

✦　✦　✦

Katharina urges Wolf to hurry. Tomorrow Anna Strauss is to be married. Anna is a young relative who has been in the house for four years and is as dear to Katharina as her own daughters. Using a fabric interwoven with gold threads, a gift to Katharina from the elector last Christmas, Anna's wedding dress is being sewn, and it needs to be finished today.

Through the old oak beside the Elster gate they see a jagged line of lightning, followed quickly by crackling thunder. Katharina and Wolf hurry to make it home without getting wet, as the first large drops announce the arrival of a welcome rain. "I hope Hänschen and Florian get through this storm," Katharina worries. Along with Lippus Melanchthon, the two boys earned their first academic degree, the baccalaureate, last year. Since then, Hänschen has been living and studying with his cousin, Florian von Bora, in Torgau at Markus Krodel's Latin school. Katharina misses her firstborn a great deal. And she knows that Magdalena, her beautiful, sweet, and gentle little daughter, can hardly wait for her brother to arrive from Torgau.

The next morning, Katharina helps Anna dress in her bridal finery. The dress is splendid, with dainty ruffles around a high, closed collar, and full sleeves along the hem of which the gold embroidery gleams.

Anna turns around and around before the mirror. Suddenly she throws her arms around Katharina. "Thank you, you are the best of all mothers!"

Oh God. Katharina knows that isn't true. How often did she scold this girl (who at sixteen resembles her outwardly, while Katharina's own daughters favor Martinus), scold her bitterly, even though from the very first she felt a great affection for this orphaned child of her cousin's. But Anna often drew Katharina's ever-ready anger, because she loves nothing more than standing in front of the mirror, trying on clothes. She'll always be arranging her hair differently, or fashioning a new schapel from flowers, ribbons, and sprigs. A blemish on her chin or forehead can drive her into deepest depression for days. In church or at the market, she has never kept her eyes to herself. Katharina has seen Christoffel and Jakob prowling around Anna. And most of all Dr. Cuckoo. (Actually, his name is Schenk, but Martinus calls him that because he disparages Luther's teachings behind his back, while outwardly acting the utterly devoted disciple.) When he asked for Anna's hand, Martinus for once was able to rein in his anger at this magister's falseness. He turned him down with clear but civil words. Katharina, by contrast, wasn't able to restrain herself from adding, "I'd never let my daughter marry a liar like you."

And with that Katharina made herself yet another enemy for life. So what? She has learned to keep malicious gossip and slander at a distance. Early in her marriage she wavered between blazing anger and blackest despair whenever she encountered either open hatred or malicious rumors. It was especially hard when she was expecting her first child. The whispering seemed to come from every quarter: "When monk and nun sleep together they beget the Antichrist." This notion became fixed in many people's imaginations when word of her pregnancy was first circulating. There were whisperings about it everywhere; even her friends didn't dare disagree. Of all people, it was Erasmus who was able to calm Katharina's fears and doubts that sometimes reached the level of panic (and Martinus had not succeeded in allaying them). Erasmus openly ridiculed the barbaric nonsense of this rumor: "If that were true, the world would be teeming with Antichrists."

Oh yes, Katharina has learned. Sometimes she tells herself that it is perhaps a blessing that comes with increasing age (which is otherwise so bothersome) that one learns to keep one's distance from people who are offensive, truly sick and malevolent. In fact, Katharina is doing much better at finding joy in the affection of others and at receiving that affection. She knows that she has few friends. So they're all the more important to her. When she thinks about her women friends, when she is around them, she finds ever greater pleasure in the feeling of acceptance and support they share. For Katharina Jonas, for Walpurga Bugenhagen, for Barbara Cranach, for Else Agricola she would not hesitate to sacrifice her last pfennig, the last bit of grain from her pantry, even her health. That last willingness in particular she has been able to demonstrate often. She, who like Martinus fears neither plague nor cholera, who really has never got either the English sweats or malaria, goes tirelessly from house to house, washing the sick, administering medicaments, tending the houseguests and the sick children at home, and meanwhile still running her ever-growing collection of properties. Sometimes it seems to Katharina that, as the demands on her grow, she is growing wings to meet them.

Then, when she sees members of the household (or the older children) idle, her anger is all the more vivid. And so it has been that Anna often became the target—for thinking only of her beauty and of her suitors while everything around her seemed to be collapsing into chaos.

But today Katharina feels only pride and joy regarding her lovely niece, who is to be wed by Martinus in the town church early this afternoon. The bridegroom, the eldest son of Bürgermeister Reichenbach, is so head over heels for Anna that lately he has been spending every free minute in the Luther house. Luther used to enjoy teasing the two of them lovingly. He even defended them before Katharina, who would sometimes grow impatient and say, "Now, there's been enough billing and cooing for one day."

At this moment Katharina regrets her vehemence. Especially because Anna is always so grateful and trusting. The girl's dark eyes shine with such assurance and joy into the mirror, it's as if they were watching and waiting for a miracle. This thought causes Katharina pain. She has never loved Anna as much as she does this instant.

Katharina looks behind Anna in the mirror. Beside the lovely, young face still untouched by life, she suddenly sees her own. How long it's been since she looked at herself! She is crestfallen. Her hair, still full and dark, has pronounced silver streaks along the sides. On her forehead, between her nose and the corners of her mouth, beneath her eyes—everywhere there are shadows and runes. Wrinkles encircle her mouth. For a second, Katharina wishes she could erase the lines that forty-two years of life have dug into her face. And pull away the pale, tired, weather-beaten skin like a mask that is merely concealing her radiantly young, true face.

Yet Katharina's grief soon gives way to a quiet melancholy that she has come to know quite well. She has found a place for it, so to speak, amid the elaborate confusion of her feelings. She notes with a sort of unconscious gratitude that life has evidently taught her the art of poking fun at herself now and then.

And so, after this brief moment of grieving, she observes that these unavoidable signs of aging don't do her much harm. After all, Martinus doesn't see very well anymore. Just yesterday he tossed his new glasses across the table with a curse: "Throw these at Christian Döring's head! He makes me such bad glasses, I see better without them!"

She ascribes it to this condition when Martinus tells her (and he says it more and more often) that she is beautiful. "My lovely morning star," he says. Then Katharina finds herself thinking that at certain times nearsightedness actually has some value. And, fortunately, what Martinus sees with his hands has not yet fallen prey to advancing age. Katharina loves her body like a reliable friend, faithful at all times. She has grown stronger, but her proportions are balanced, her bosom is full and beautiful. Even in days of misery, when illness, death, and worries make the Black Cloister into a haven of ill temper and crisis, even at her lowest point, Katharina can pull herself back up with the thought that sometime (even when the days are blurring together) she will prepare herself a bath of flower petals and rose oil.

And she knows why that is so. Because it gives her pleasure to care for her skin and hair. And the greatest pleasure it arouses is her desire for Martinus. And he has long since realized that he cannot do without this desire. While he may set his will against hers by day (if only to save face before the others), at night he is at her mercy. Sooner or later her pleading, her crying, her cajoling always become the familiar sounds of their shared desire, which comes as surely as the dawn of each new day.

Just as Martinus lives with many afflictions authored by the Devil, he has grown to accept that the pleasure of the senses comes at a price. And since he knows that this cannot remain hidden from anyone in the house, he anticipates any possible commentary, saying to Katharina at table, for example, "You talk me into whatever you want. Your authority is absolute. In the household I accede authority to you, my own rights notwithstanding . . ."

Once he welcomes a new guest by saying, "Accept the welcome of a humble host, for he is obedient unto the women." And he introduces Katharina: "I am the underlord, she is the overlord; I am the Aaron, she is my Moses . . ."

"Mother, should we knot my hair beneath the veil, or should it hang down long?"

Katharina has been so immersed in her thoughts that she hasn't even noticed how Anna keeps trying on her veil, tying her hair up, combing it out again, braiding it, loosening the braids. Finally they decide to let the hair hang down simply beneath a wreath of blossoms. Katharina has another idea. She brings her golden chain, a gift from the princess of Anhalt, whom Katharina attended in the Black Cloister during an outbreak of cholera two years ago. She puts this chain on the bride. Martinus has joined them unnoticed: "People used to take their gold to the churches; now evidently they wear it all around their necks."

He is in good spirits. As is always the case when he can do something for others. For the wedding banquet he has spared no expense. A fat buck is roasting in the baking oven, and there is plenty of Franconian wine for the great host of guests that Martinus has invited.

Everyone in the Black Cloister is dressed for the occasion. Wolf Sieberger and Katharina have tied colorful bouquets for the bride and the other girls. It is a festive scene as the wedding party sets out for the church. Hans and Magdalena, the eldest of the Luther children, follow the bride and groom. With her white dress and gaily colored schapel, Magdalena looks like a bride. And the fifteen-year-old Hans, with his close-fitting leggings and dark green doublet complete with belt and sword, looks quite grown up. Katharina exchanges a glance with Martinus, who has also been sneaking a look at his eldest children. Both Martinus and Katharina are thinking the same thing: "Hänschen and Lenichen—they're almost more beautiful than the bride and groom . . ."

During the whole wedding celebration brother and sister are inseparable. They know that Hans (and his cousin Florian with him) must soon return to Torgau.

12

An icy wind sweeps through the streets and alleyways of Wittenberg. It is dark and still; only in the Black Cloister is a light burning. Katharina is working quietly in the kitchen. She is preparing a chest tonic for Martinus, who is again having difficulty breathing. Katharina has everything she needs at hand: spleenwort, hyssop, dates, figs, anise and fennel seeds. She adds them all to a pound and a half of water, which she boils down to one-sixth the original volume. When Martinus drinks some of this, he feels better. She always keeps a chest salve ready. It is made of almond oil, unsalted butter, saffron, and wax, to be heated and spread on the chest and back.

As Katharina carefully applies the hot salve, Martinus groans. "You'll see, soon I'll lie down in my coffin and the maggots will have a fat doctor to eat."

Katharina is used to hearing Martinus refer to himself as a bag of maggots or mouse droppings. Not even the festering sores on his leg does he take seriously. While Katharina is washing the leg down with chamomile water and covering it with a cool salve, Martinus remarks that envy is ever on the increase in this world. "Now that I have an open leg, Justus Jonas will have to rush out and get one for himself."

Relieved that Martinus is getting air enough to feel like joking again, Katharina gets back into bed. In the silence, she hears her heart beating. The sounds of the house reach her, familiar and comforting in the all-encompassing darkness. She thinks she can hear the children whispering in their dreams. And the thought crosses her mind that all life that is conceived comes from the darkness. Why then are we still so afraid of the dark?

Just then Martinus says, "Katharina, have Philippus, Kaspar, and Johannes come here tomorrow. I want to make my will."

For a moment Katharina's heart stops. She feels as if death were slipping in from the dark corners of the room and sitting down, with a grin, right on her chest. She presses herself close to Martinus. But this time the warmth of his skin cannot calm her. Anxiously she lies beside him, one hand on his chest. The beat of his pulse just increases the trembling of her own heart.

The next day, Martinus is still weak, but he insists nevertheless on having his three closest friends come. And they do write their names beneath his last will and testament, in which he bequeaths to Katharina the estate at Zulsdorf, all goblets and jewels, rings, chains, and so forth.

Martinus spells out his reasons:

> . . . because as a pious, faithful, honest spouse, she has always loved, cherished, and been good to me, and through God's abundant blessing has borne and raised five living children . . .
>
> . . . because she will assume and pay the remaining

debts I have not paid off during my lifetime, I being aware of some 450 gulden in debts, but others might be found as well . . .

. . . because I wish the children to look to her for support, and not the other way around. I believe that she will be the best guardian for her children and will use her goods and property in the best interest of the children she once carried under her heart . . .

. . . and I herewith implore my Lord Duke Johannes Friedrich, His Grace the Elector, to protect and enforce this, my gift or bequest . . .

. . . I also ask all my good friends to be witnesses on behalf of my dear Katharina and to help her if any useless gossips should burden or slander her . . .

Katharina's anxiety over Martinus's evident fear or premonition of death does not abate until she sees him begin, day by day, to devote himself more to his Reformationist efforts and affairs. Sometimes, when she is able to look up from her own domestic confusion, fears, struggles, and crises, it seems to her that the world outside is in confusion far greater than her own.

France has allied with Turkey, with the Pope secretly joining the alliance. And fighting against the Pope—with the support of the Protestant princes—is the emperor. They fight for this emperor, of all people, even though he is determined to eradicate heresy once and for all. Katharina can make no sense of it all.

In England, King Henry VIII, who once mocked Katharina's and Martinus's marriage, has drawn a line between

England and Rome by marrying Anne Boleyn. Martinus, who is consulted on the matter, is outraged at Henry's repudiation of Queen Catherine and says so openly, which of course the English king holds against him.

But far worse are the sufferings Martinus and Melanchthon endure over the Landgrave of Hessen's double marriage. The emperor blackmails him for the capital crime of bigamy. In the Schmalkaldic League, which strengthened the Reformation, the landgrave (to save his own neck) now represents the interests of the emperor. The reformist currents that spilled over into Sweden, Denmark, and France are dried up by force of arms. The emperor has the Protestants in his hand. And so they do not rally around the Duke of Cleves when he gets into a war against the emperor.

Blood and violence yet again. War. Will it come to Wittenberg as well? The city is more and more fortified. Many outsiders come in with the construction crews.

Prostitutes, too, have moved in. From the pulpit, Martinus pours out his anger, which is actually directed at the goings-on (especially those of the students) in Wittenberg in general: "Our gracious lord did not found this university for whores' beds or brothels. For it cannot be calculated what damage such lewd whores cause among young people. A single French whore can poison ten, twenty, thirty, a hundred children of good people before they're even really men. The young gentlemen think that as soon as they feel the rutting urge, they should go find a whore."

Katharina can hardly wait for the sermon to end. For one thing, she is not especially interested in what the whores are up to. She is much more worried about Magdalena. Her older daughter has been home in bed for several days, feeling tired and weak. At first, Katharina thought Magdalena was having her first menses. But she has none of the other symptoms. Finally, Katharina called Dr. Schurf. He tested and probed Magdalena, but said he couldn't really tell what was bothering her. In any case, they should give her the milk of a nursing she-donkey or fresh goat's milk. But Magdalena, who usually is obedient in all things, will not drink either one. Not even when, on the advice of Dr. Schurf, Katharina adds rose sugar to the milk.

When Magdalena spits up blood one evening, they all know that it's her lungs.

✦   ✦   ✦

For Katharina, it's as if a dense haze now blankets every day. The closer she sees death coming for Magdalena, the more feverishly Katharina clings to the rituals of life. Again and again, she rubs her daughter's back and chest with sweet almond oil. She boils her a syrup of licorice, hyssop, gum arabic, and barley water. She tries to entice Magdalena to eat by cooking her the finest capons, hulled barley, almond milk, egg yolks, veal or baby goat. Although she knows that her child's hours are numbered, she cooks and brews as if by doing so she could keep death away from Magdalena's bed.

Then she sits by the bed, trying to fix every minute, every breath, every sound of her daughter's voice in her memory, as if she could hold on to life this way. Once,

Magdalena says, "It's so nice, Mother, being sick."

"Why is it nice, Lenichen?"

"Because, Mother, you are with me so much."

That hits Katharina like a physical blow. When, yes, when did she last spend time with Magdalena? What, besides pride in her beauty, has she ever felt for her daughter? When was the last time she reflected on Magdalena's dreams? What has she known of her child's life? What does she know of Hans, of Martin, of Paul, what does she know of little Maruschel and the adopted children? Only that they need to be fed and clothed, obedient, and attentive to their studies. Overcome with guilt, Katharina has just one wish: if only she could read what was behind her child's ever-more-pallid forehead. Has Magdalena been cheerful in her life? What has made her happy, what fears has she endured?

Magdalena. In despair, Katharina reaches both arms around her daughter. The girl sits up, speaks: "I would like to see Hänsichen one more time."

Martinus, who until now has not believed she was in serious danger, writes immediately to Markus Krodel in Torgau: "Magdalena so longs to see her brother that I must send the wagon for him. They love each other so. It could be that his coming might restore her strength."

Hans arrives in Wittenberg, and that same night Katharina dreams that two handsome noblemen have come to ask for Magdalena's hand. The one she chooses is to lead her to the altar.

Katharina awakens from this dream happy. When Melanchthon arrives early in the morning to look in on Magdalena, she tells him the dream. She sees Melanchthon pale; horrified, she races to Magdalena's bed. She realizes suddenly what her dream means: two angels are taking Magdalena home.

On the evening of this day, the twentieth of September, 1542, Magdalena dies. Her brother, Hans, holds her in his arms. Martinus buries his head in his hands and sobs out loud.

Katharina feels nothing. She hears and sees as if through a fog that the room is filling with people who are close to her. They are all there, but Katharina's stony silence is so palpable that none, not even Barbara, Walpurga, or Melanchthon, dares approach her.

She hears Martinus beginning to speak: "Ach, dear Lenchen, you will rise again and shine like a star, yes, like the sun. My daughter is in good hands now. We know that it must be so. We Christians are assured of eternal life. Two saints God has taken from my flesh. Elisabeth and Magdalena . . ."

Stop it! Is Katharina thinking this, or is she screaming it out loud? Stop it! Stop it!

Although she knows that Martinus is talking to save his life, that he's talking and talking so as not to lose his mind, although she understands his helpless despair, she still wants to shake him and scream that he should stop all this babbling. God, God, God! Is there a God?

Katharina remains motionless as they bring the coffin. It is white, and much too short for Lenichen. Once the dead child is lying inside the coffin with legs drawn up, Martinus falls silent as well.

Everyone leaves but Hans. He lights thirteen candles around his sister's coffin. Then he, too, leaves.

Martinus and Katharina stand alone in the bedroom. Mute and distant from each another. Like two pillars, thinks Katharina. Like two pillars in the vault of death.

13

———

The morning is sunny, though the trees are still bare and gray. Katharina has put some twigs into water; in the warm room their buds have begun to open, and the tips are a delicate green.

It's time for church. The bells have begun tolling. Katharina wraps a warm shawl around Maruschel-Margarete, for the church will be cold. Paulus and Martin too are to take their warm doublets. The brilliant sun is deceptive.

Barbara is already seated in her pew. So are Walpurga and her children. For a moment, Katharina puts her arms around Margarete, who no longer wants to be called Maruschel. In church, she finally has time to sit back and just look at her children. Everyone says that Margarete-Maruschel, Katharina's sole remaining daughter, resembles her mother more and more every day. She's ten now. She has dark, thick hair (Martinus's hair), which frames her face with an abundance of waves and curls. She is tall, and her face—with her light skin, dark, fine eyebrows and slightly asymmetrical eyes—is strikingly attractive. Paulus, sitting with the boys on the other side, his eyes restlessly wandering around the room, resembles his younger sister the most. But Martin is a different type altogether: he's blond, with bright eyes and a rather pronounced nose, which, despite his thirteen-year-old manliness, he is all too fond of picking. Which is what he's doing now.

The congregation sings the second stanza of the hymn by Elisabeth Cruziger:

> A child born to us
> In the last part of time
> So that we shall not be lost
> In God's eternity
> Released us from Death's chains
> Unlocked the gates of Heaven
> Returned to us our life.

Since Lenichen's death, Katharina has often thought about Elisabeth Cruziger, who died ten years ago. She wasn't even thirty years old. How happy she was to finally be pregnant. And then she paid for the miscarriage with her life. Elisabeth, dear talented friend. And a little later, the pain over her loss was increased when Aunt Lene, too, took to her bed and never recovered.

Katharina has come to have many graves to visit in the cemetery by the Elster gate. Lenichen. Every feature of her face, every word from her lips, her every gesture—each is so deeply etched into Katharina's memory that she can never forget it.

Just yesterday, Martinus wrote to Nikolaus Amsdorf: "How the death of my Magdalena torments me. I cannot forget her."

Her gravestone reads:

> Here I sleep, Lenichen, Dr. Luther's little girl
> Resting now with all the saints, in my little bed
> I was born in sin
> And would surely have been lost
> But now I am alive and well
> Lord Christ, redeemed by your blood

Now Martinus steps up to the pulpit, turns the pages of his Bible, joins in singing the last lines of the stanza:

> . . . direct our hearts to You
> And turn us from our senses
> That they may not lead away from You.

Martinus's Epistle reading is from the Letter to the Ephesians, the fifth chapter. "Therefore, dear brothers, be imitators of God as beloved children . . ."

Katharina's thoughts are wandering again. She is often unable to concentrate on the liturgy. Still, she often finds a certain relief here from the toils and strains of her daily life. Here she can gather her energies, although sometimes she thinks she keeps coming only to fulfill a duty.

Martinus is reading: ". . . Be sure of this, that no fornicator or impure person, or one who is greedy (that is, an idolater), has any inheritance in the kingdom of Christ and of God. Let no one deceive you with empty words, for because of these things the wrath of God comes on the children of disobedience. Therefore do not be associated with them . . . Live as children of light—for the fruit of the light is found in all that is good and right and true."

Children of disobedience. Why is it that more and more often lately Katharina has had a sense of disquiet—of constant, restless change? Nothing stays. Beloved people are ripped away. Word of new deaths comes often to the Black Cloister. Katharina Jonas, whose move to Halle caused Katharina great pain, died during the Christmas holidays last year. Barbara Cranach grows ever more silent and withdrawn. Only Walpurga and Ave in faraway Berlin are left of Katharina's circle of friends. She has lost dear, gentle Else Agricola because Agricola became irreconcilably alienated from Martinus over matters of faith.

That is one reason why Martinus has grown so mistrustful of late, so somber, so irritable. Out of pity he took in a couple of refugees a few weeks ago, as he has done so often before. They said they were a brother and sister named Truchsess from Münnerstadt in Franconia. Persecuted and slandered on account of their Protestant faith. Might Dr. Luther take them into his service? No job would be too menial for them.

After only a few days of false piety, the two stole everything out of the Black Cloister that they could carry. All the money, coins, goblets, jewelry. They figured out where things were kept and then took them at night. Martinus immediately sent out riders in pursuit. So far to no avail.

✦　✦　✦

And Wittenberg itself. Martinus has had his fill of the city. When he was in Leipzig four weeks ago, he wrote:

I would be glad if I could arrange never to need to return to Wittenberg. My heart has grown cold, so that I no longer like being there; I wish, too, that you would sell garden, hoof, house, and hearth. I for my part would gladly give back the Black Cloister to my most gracious lord. It would be best for you if you settled in Zulsdorf while I am still alive. I could still help you with my salary to put the estate into better condition. After my death, the four elements probably will not tolerate your staying in Wittenberg. So it is better that what needs doing be done during my lifetime. As it is run now Wittenberg may be headed not for a St. Vitus's dance but for more like a beggar's dance or a dance with the Devil, as they have begun exposing women and maidens, both front and back, and there is no one to punish it and keep order. And the Word of God is being mocked. Let us be gone from this Sodom. I have heard more in the countryside than I ever learn in Wittenberg. And so I am tired of the city and do not wish to return.

What if Martinus really doesn't return to Wittenberg? Zulsdorf . . . that might be well and good to sustain the family and the purse, but otherwise—the nights there are as dull and drab as the days.

Katharina went directly to Melanchthon and showed him the letter. He in turn consulted with Bugenhagen. Then the university officially appealed to the elector, who immediately dispatched Dr. Ratzeberger with a letter to Martinus. From the Council of the City of Wittenberg, Bürgermeister Gregor Mathes and the city magistrate and book printer Hans Lufft set off for Leipzig to see Luther. Together with Melanchthon, Bugenhagen, and Cruziger, they were able to persuade him to return to Wittenberg.

✦   ✦   ✦

Katharina looks at Martinus as he stands in the pulpit and preaches the Gospel. She has still not quite got used to the idea that the man who held her in heated embrace during the night is now standing up there and proclaiming the Word of God. He is reading from Luke, the eleventh chapter: "Now he was casting out a demon that was mute; when the demon had gone out, the one who had been mute spoke, and the crowds were amazed . . . But Jesus said to them, 'Every kingdom divided against itself becomes a desert, and house falls on house.' "

Both the Epistle and the Gospel remain in Katharina's thoughts for a long while.

> . . . the children of disobedience . . .
> . . . house falls on house . . .

That night, Katharina dreams of a great city at the foot of rolling blue hills, a city in the fog, its rooftops and parapets gleaming red, violet or blue. A fine golden glow shimmers over the whole of it. A lovely city; a splendid city. Only one house (is it the Black Cloister?) has lost half its roof. But the ruins, overgrown with ivy, gleam in the same golden light as the other houses. Then, a great, splendid procession! Cistercian monks carry the banner, swing the incense burners. Walking behind them are the Reverend Mother and Father Abbot Peter von der Pforte. Even in her dream,

Katharina knows that they have both been dead for ten years. Next comes Sebastian Franck, the writer, dancing and shrieking mockingly, "We are all laughter, fable, and Shrovetide farce before God!" He is followed by priests of the old faith in full clerical vestments. Beneath a canopy they carry the Most Holy Sacrament. Then come troops of bishops; they must be from Münster. They are carrying the three iron cages with the Baptists in them that hang from the Lamberti Tower in Münster. Alongside Jan von Leiden, Krechting, and Knipperdolling, who hang horribly mutilated in their cages, Martinus, Philippus, Bugenhagen, and Cruziger are on display, fettered and emasculated, also in cages. The soldiers reach into the cages with red-hot tongs. Again and again. After them comes the Pope in his purple mantle and golden tiara, escorted by six cardinals. Beside the Pope, the Duke of Braunschweig. Katharina thinks with a pang of fear that Martinus just recently called him an uncouth clod, dolt and oaf, the donkey of all the donkeys in Wolfenbüttel. He refers to the Pope exclusively as Pope-donkey and the Roman church as whorehouse or Devil's church.

Katharina tries to hide herself and the children behind all the people watching the procession, but the Pope has seen them. He points at them, and so does the duke: "*The children of disobedience, the children of disobedience!*"

Katharina finally awakens with a scream. She is bathed in sweat and feels numb. It's only three in the morning, but under no circumstances does she want to go back to sleep and have more dreams. She gets up and starts a fire in the stove for a bath.

14

WITTENBERG, JANUARY 10, 1546

It is winter again, and a rather mild day. Snowflakes are dancing, falling thick and fast. They cover the already whitened houses and streets with merciless silence and determination.

In the courtyard of the Black Cloister a sleigh stands waiting. The breath of the four draft horses billows away in clouds. Their hooves paw the ground; they toss their heads back.

Martinus is going to his hometown, Mansfeld. The counts of Mansfeld have called on him to mediate an inheritance conflict.

Katharina thinks Martinus looks good in his black coat lined with fox fur, over a doublet of dark camlet with lapels of satin. Hans, Martin, and Paul also have fur-lined coats. They are looking forward to the journey. But Margarete is shivering as she clings to her mother.

Martinus and the boys climb aboard the sleigh. Katharina carefully tucks in the sheepskins around their legs. In a second sleigh, Johann Aurifaber and Johann Rudtfeld, the house tutor, are ready to go. Justus Jonas will join them in Halle. Katharina sends along no greeting for him. She cannot forget that only three months after the death of his wife, Katharina, he remarried.

Katharina urges Martinus to take care of himself: "I'm worried, Martinus."

He laughs. "You think *you* should worry about me instead of your God? As if he weren't almighty enough to make ten Dr. Martinuses if the old one kicked off by falling into the Saale, or into the stove for that matter . . . or into Wolf's bird trap . . . leave me in peace with your worrying."

He leans over for a fleeting kiss. The sons call out, "Hya! Hya!" The horses toss their heads back, and quickly the sleigh glides out of the courtyard.

Katharina stands in the gate, holding Margarete by the hand. She watches the sled until Margarete says, "I'm so cold, Mother."

✦　　✦　　✦

Wittenberg, the night of February 21–22, 1546
Katharina is sitting at Martinus's desk. Without solace she writes page after page.

Grace and Peace in Christ, dearest Ave. In the stillness of this night I am writing to you. Martinus is dead. He journeyed to his hometown to die there. He did not want to do it in Wittenberg. And not with me. He has left me, Ave.

My Hans, my Martin, and my Paulus were with him in his last hour. Justus Jonas was there, and it is from him that I received word. Magister Cölius and Johann Aurifaber saw him draw his last breath. The innkeeper Johann Albrecht, two doctors from the town, Count Albrecht with his wife, Count Heinrich von Schwarzenberg, also with his wife. And they called in Furtennagel, the painter. They all were there with him. Only I was not.

I still have letters from him, Ave. From February first, from the sixth, from the seventh, from the tenth, from the fourteenth . . . Ach, Ave. He calls me his tenderly beloved housewife, Doktorin, Zulsdörferin, Saumärkterin, self-martyrer (because I worried on his account). To my gracious Lady's hands and feet, he writes . . .

To the profoundly learned Lady Katherin Lutherin of the Holy, Diligent Ladies, Your Holiness's willing servant—he wrote me all that, Ave. And believe me, I have been all of that for him.

Your old sweetheart—he writes that, too, and he was my sweetheart, as surely as there is a God.

And now, Ave?

We are beggars, that is true. Martinus wrote it before he died. Justus Jonas told me so.

Believe me, Ave, until now every day, no matter how dark, how painful it might have been (and only you know what times I mean in particular), every one of these days has been in spite of everything a promise of another day to come.

Now that Martinus has left me, nothing awaits me tomorrow. I loved him, Ave. But our feelings always stayed hidden behind our everyday words, our work, our quarreling.

But now, Ave, now I would like to say it to him. I

would like to let him know that every time my hand touched and caressed the head of one of our children, in truth I was caressing his head, his face. Alongside every hard word I spoke to him was also my plea: come to me, talk with me, take me as seriously as you do your friends and your enemies.

Into every loaf of bread I baked, Ave, I kneaded my love for him.

And when I brewed beer, my thought was that it should taste good to him.

And when I added onto the cloister, ever more and ever larger, I did it so that Martinus's guests could live here.

And when I sowed seed and threshed wheat, it was so that Martinus would have bread and porridge.

You ask me, Ave, why I didn't say this to him?

I didn't fully realize it until just now.

Now it is morning, Ave, not light yet, but still morning. The candles are still burning. Did I fall asleep for a while?

It's time to bring this letter to a close, Ave.

Furtennagel, the painter, has thrown clay onto Martinus's face. He is making a death mask of him. That, too, was in Justus Jonas's letter. The count of Mansfeld is sending one hundred and thirteen riders to escort Martinus from Eisleben to Wittenberg.

Ave, now I hear the bells of the castle church. And now those of the town church.

Ave, they're bringing him.

Ave, I'm afraid . . .